M. McLaren Cunningham

THE BOOK THAT SPI

THE
BOOK THAT SPEAKS
FOR ITSELF

ROBERT M. HORN

INTER-VARSITY PRESS

INTER-VARSITY PRESS

Inter-Varsity Fellowship
39 Bedford Square, London WC1

Inter-Varsity Christian Fellowship
130 north Wells, Chicago, Illinois 60606

© INTER-VARSITY PRESS, LONDON
First Edition May 1969

UK STANDARD BOOK NUMBER 85110 345 6

Biblical quotations are from the Revised Standard Version, copyrighted
1946 and 1952

PRINTED AND BOUND IN ENGLAND BY
HAZELL WATSON AND VINEY LTD
AYLESBURY, BUCKS

CONTENTS

INTRODUCTION

ACCUMULATING DUST ON A SHELF, the Bible certainly looks dull and harmless enough. Maybe it is the world's best-seller, but it sometimes seems to be the least read. Looking at it, you would never guess the energy that has been expended on it. Lives given to translate, print, spread and teach it. Efforts made to destroy, burn, criticize and demolish it. And the influence it has exerted on people and cultures over the centuries is staggering.

All this is, of course, a matter of fact : most would agree that the Bible is a unique book. But why prolong debate about it? In view of the conflicts about it, why not call a truce? Discussion has not dispelled confusion. So we should let the dust settle, and everyone can believe what seems right to them. For the sake of peace and charity, let the matter rest.

Yet would that be peace – or the peace of death? Is my assessment of the Bible in fact the crucial factor? Is it true that, once my judgment is formed, there is no more to be said to me? If the Bible is actually God's voice to men, as it claims to be, then the positions are reversed : my opinion of the Bible is secondary to the Bible's opinion of me. What matters ultimately is not how I judge the Bible, but how its Author judges me. A greater issue is at stake than my private thoughts about a collection of books.

There are signs, too, that some are again beginning to take sober account of the Bible. For a long period everybody who was anybody (or thought to be) discounted the Bible's historicity and message. Ronald Knox's satirical character the Bishop of Much Wenlock was not alone in proceeding on the dictum that 'Facts are only the steam which obscures the mirror of truth'.[1] Now some in the realm of biblical research have felt themselves compelled by facts to reassert the Bible as history. Many in the realm of conduct have re-established for themselves the Bible's standards. Others have concluded that the emasculated Christianity bequeathed by some critics of the Bible was both groundless and pointless.

No. The Bible cannot simply be ignored. It demands to be taken seriously.

[1] *Essays in Satire*, p. 177.

CHAPTER ONE

APPROACHING THE BIBLE

THE BIBLE has been called God's word, His autobiography. People may query or deny whether this is so; but if it is, the matter is vital and urgent. The questions we must face therefore are these : What sort of a book is the Bible? What is its nature, authority, function? And as soon as we face these, others crop up : Where do we begin to look at the Bible? How do we approach it?

This last question may sound odd. Surely we just pick up the Bible and read it with due care and attention. After all, the Bible is a collection of books, and books are meant to be read. This is how we would start on Shakespeare or William Golding. So we should begin to study the Bible as we would any other example of ancient literature : look at its historical and geographical background, the literary form of its component books. This all sounds too obvious to need stating at all. The question 'where to begin?' is redundant.

This is fine. No-one should be discouraged from simply getting a Bible and starting to read it. Far better to read the Bible than any number of books about the Bible! There is no better way of finding out what Christianity actually says. But the difficulty is in being open-minded to what the Bible says. For instance, to approach the Bible as a collection of merely human writings is to approach it with a prejudgment concerning the nature of the book and the ways of God. To presuppose that it is merely human is to presuppose that it is not a book of divine origin. To presuppose this is to believe beforehand that God did not give this as His personal self-disclosure. You may think it a right presupposition; it is a presupposition nonetheless. And presuppositions have a strange habit of reappearing in conclusions.

To ask therefore, 'Where should we begin in approaching the Bible?' is simply to acknowledge that we all have our own ideas about God already. We all start from somewhere when we consider Him, and we bring this starting point with us when we look at Scripture. Stated in its simplest terms, it comes to this : our view of God determines our view of Scripture. Let me illustrate.

To put it at its most obvious, a person who denies God's existence will not subscribe to belief in the Bible.

A Muslim, convinced that God cannot beget, will not accept as the Word of God a book that teaches that Christ is the only begotten Son of God.

Some believe that God is not personal, but rather the Ultimate, the Ground of Being. Such will be predisposed to reject the Bible as God's personal self-revelation. On their premises, the Bible cannot be the personal word of 'I AM WHO I AM' (Ex. 3 : 14).

Others rule out the supernatural. They will not be likely to give credence to the book which teaches that Christ rose from the dead.

Still others hold that God cannot communicate His truth undistorted through sinful men; hence they regard the Bible as, at least in parts, no more than human.

But if you believe that God is personal, living, the God of the supernatural; if you are persuaded that He reigns and is able to do as He wills, then you will not find it so hard to be open to the actual facts concerning the Bible.

Every differing view of the Bible arises from a differing view of God. When we come to consider the Bible therefore, the question we face is the question of God Himself. We are not engaged simply in literary criticism or archaeological investigation. The fact of the Bible forces us to ask : what is my attitude to God Himself?

All this affects the approach of this present book. I shall not try to argue towards a certain view of the Bible from the position of someone who is not convinced of the living God. Such a process is eminently possible, of course. Many lines of evidence exist which do in fact show the Bible to be God's unique self-revelation. Such evidence is part of the rational basis for believing in the Bible. But to start here is to put the cart before the horse. Belief in God as the Father of Jesus Christ comes first, logically and experimentally. Certainly the truths in Scripture are what the Spirit uses to bring people to God. But true convictions concerning the nature of the Bible itself begin to take shape within a personal relationship with God in Christ.

So we must start with God.

GOD AND THE BIBLE

Christ and the writers of Scripture never try to prove the existence of God. This is significant. The very idea is ridiculous to them. God *is*, whether or not the fool says in his heart, 'There is no God' (Ps. 14 : 1). God is not for proof but proclamation; not for argument, but acceptance. He is the great I AM. He is the living One. God's 'as I live' affirms that His existence is the one fact in the universe that is axiomatic. This does not in the least mean that belief in God is irrational; it merely underlines two facts :

First, *the inadequacy of 'proofs'*. The deity who emerges from proofs is little more than a Prime Mover, a First Cause, an Absolute. This is not the personal God of the Bible, not the Father of the Lord Jesus Christ, not the God of resurrection. In any case, 'to demonstrate conclusively that God exists, you would have to find something more ultimate than him, from which his existence could be shown to be necessarily derived. And that is, from the very nature of the case, impossible; for God is ... the *ultimate*'.[1]

Second, *the state of men's minds*. Men are blind to spiritual truth and rebels against God. Because they do not want the truth about God, they will not be moved to trade in their antipathy by proofs, however convincing in themselves. A man convinced against his will is of the same opinion still. Their minds first need to be enlightened; only then do they begin to see straight in relation to God.

In the following chapters, therefore, we shall try to show how a true view of God must affect our approach to the Bible. For the Christian, the follower of Christ, it is His example that is supremely relevant. We willingly accept His right to teach us about our duty to love God and our neighbour; He has equal right to teach us about the nature of Scripture. And it is clear from a welter of explicit statements and incidental allusions that He regarded the Old Testament (His Bible) as the inspired Word of His Father. To Him it was trustworthy and authoritative, the source of all true awareness of God and His will.[2] To Him 'it is written' was an end of argument. He obeyed the Old Testament because He saw it as His Father's word. When He quoted from it to the Sadducees, He introduced the words of Exodus 3 :6 by the question : 'have you not read what was said to you by God?' (Mt. 22 :31). On other occasions when He asked, 'Have you not read (the Old Testament)?' He was assuming that those who had this book should know that it was His Father's truth.[3]

---

[1] Michael Green, *Choose Freedom*, p. 14.
[2] See J. W. Wenham, *Our Lord's View of the Old Testament*.
[3] *Cf.* Mt. 12 :3,5; 19 :4; 21 :16,42; and parallels.

Such instances are not isolated, freak phenomena, but integral to His whole life and outlook. His view of His Father could lead Him only to this view of Scripture. As God's only Son, He gladly acknowledged the written Scripture as the Word of God. His view of God determined His view of this book. It should be the same for us.

'A disciple is not above his teacher' (Mt. 10 : 24).

So we must now turn to examine how we come to know God.

CHAPTER TWO

CAN WE KNOW GOD?

WE HAVE ARGUED that we must think straight about God before we can do so about the Bible. We have now to go on to say that, if the Bible is right, we can get a true view of God only from the Bible. This does not mean we lack clear evidence for His existence elsewhere, for example in the whole created order, in history and in Christian experience. But in the last analysis God authenticates Himself.

We cannot prove God by anything else simply because God is God, not man 'writ large'. By definition God is above us in every way, not spatially but morally and spiritually. He is not the end-product of a process of unaided human reasoning. He is more than the projection of man's mind and wishes. Man cannot by searching find out God (Jb. 11 :7). As Isaiah wrote (55 :8, 9) :

'For my thoughts are not your thoughts,
    neither are your ways my ways, says the Lord.
For as the heavens are higher than the earth,
    so are my ways higher than your ways
    and my thoughts than your thoughts.'

This does not make the idea of God irrational and the fact of God unreal. God is and must be His own proof – a circular argument if you like, but if God be God no other option exists. We come to know Him not primarily because of external proofs but because He opens our eyes to

14

see His testimony to Himself in Scripture. Our knowledge of God will never get off the ground until we appreciate His otherness, His Godness.

GOD IS UNKNOWABLE

This is why the historical facts are so important. God speaks to Abraham, to Moses. He gives His Word to the prophets. He sends His Son into the world. Christ spends much time teaching and preaching. Then God speaks through the apostles. He gives us Scripture. Why? Are these flamboyant but irrelevant gestures? No. He did these things because otherwise no man could ever have known God. Even today, when these facts are unknown or denied, men are still ignorant of God — hence the continuing urgency of evangelism and missionary work.

God is incomprehensible, unknowable. This does not mean that no-one has ever had a single true thought about God. It underlines the fact that no-one can ever come unaided to a true knowledge of God's nature and being and ways. For 'knowing God' means having a right relationship with Him based on the truth about Him. God alone is able to deal with man's ignorance and impart knowledge of Himself. Similarly He alone is able to deal with man's sin and give His fellowship to sinners. The otherness of God shows the necessity of divine revelation.

GOD IS PERSONAL

The fact that God is personal underscores this. You can do various things to get to know another person. You can observe his actions and behaviour, his habits and haunts. You can test his IQ or assess him psychologically. This will give you information. But by these approaches you may not come anywhere near him as a person. A person is known as he chooses to be known. This is why a husband and wife know each other so deeply and intimately. They open their hearts to each other on everything; they do not hide themselves from each other or wear masks.

If therefore you can only know me, your fellow finite being, as I reveal myself, then certainly you can only know God as He chooses to reveal Himself. Divine revelation is necessary because God is personal. This is why, to take just one line of evidence in Scripture, God reveals His names. Names then were not the nice-sounding but empty symbols they are today. Through His names God let Himself be known as everlasting, most high, the God who sees.

An outstanding example of God revealing His character through His name comes in Exodus 6:2, 3. J. A. Motyer gives the thrust of the passage by translating it as follows: 'And God spoke to Moses, and said to him: I am Yahweh. And I showed myself to Abraham, to Isaac, and to Jacob in the character of El Shaddai, but in the character expressed by my name Yahweh I did not make myself known to them.'[1] The patriarchs had known that El Shaddai stood for 'the God who takes over human incapacity and transforms it'. They had also known the name Yahweh, but not its import. Now, just as He was about to lead them out of bondage, God was ushering His people into an awareness of what *this* name enshrined. It signified in fact His acts of salvation and judgment in the Exodus, which would bring them to 'know that I am Yahweh your God' (Ex. 6:6ff.). Thus the names of God disclose and characterize His true being, His nature and thoughts and deeds.

[1] *The Revelation of the Divine Name*, p. 12.

CAN WE KNOW GOD?

So far we have thought of God as unknowable; but think also of ourselves. According to Genesis 2 :15–17 there were clear limits to man's knowledge of God apart from and prior to the fact of his sin. But now man's state as a sinner is superimposed on his status as a creature. Now he is wilfully and culpably ignorant of God. 'Light has come into the world, and men loved darkness rather than light, because their deeds were evil' (Jn. 3 :19). Man is impotent to comprehend God, for his mind is blinded (2 Cor. 4 :4).

We therefore depend absolutely on God if ever we are to know Him. We cannot hope to discover God from our side. He must come to us if ever we are to find Him. If we forget that God is incomprehensible, our thinking about revelation will run aground. We will credit too much to our own powers or our religious experience. Our need of revelation is like our need of redemption : it is total.

Yet God has provided for both needs. His self-disclosure is bound into His saving purposes. His revelation has this specific content and design. Christ came into the world to seek and to save the lost. Paul wrote that the Scriptures were able 'to instruct you for salvation through faith in Christ Jesus' (2 Tim. 3 :15). Revelation and redemption run together : this is brought out in Hebrews 1 :1–4 : 'In many and various ways God spoke of old . . . but in these last days he has spoken to us (revelation) by a Son, who . . . made purification for sins (redemption).'

The position is this : if God does not reveal and redeem, human ignorance and guilt will never be remedied. Yet our need does not put God under pressure. His freedom in this is absolute. He is not bound to reveal Himself to men who reject Him. And if He is pleased to do so, it is for Him alone to determine the content, form, timing and extent of His self-disclosure. Man fancies that he can start arguments with God on what He has or has not unveiled. His part is rather to receive intelligently, rationally and responsively God's free and sovereign revelation. Apart from God man is utterly stranded, stuck fast in his darkness and sin. In this situation it is the glory of Christianity that God is the God and Father of Christ – that is, the God who both speaks and saves. How then has He made Himself known?

REVELATION IN GENERAL

The revelation of the one God has two aspects : general and special. This may seem at first sight a nice, traditional but needless distinction. Before examining the arguments, however, what does this distinction mean?

General revelation refers to what God reveals of Himself through the universe He has made. It is a limited revelation of His invisible nature, of His eternal power and deity (Rom. 1 :20). It is general in three senses : first, it was never restricted to one group or people, but is absolutely universal; second, it does not involve God speaking personally; and third, it does not of itself lead to salvation.

Special revelation, by contrast, concerns what God has done and spoken for man's redemption in and through Christ. The distinction is between general truth and saving truth.

We hope to show that this is a biblical distinction. It is not a matter of splitting theological hairs, but is highly relevant among other things to evangelism and our thinking about non-Christians. To anticipate the argument, what Scripture says about this means that no-one is neutral towards God. Left to himself, no-one is an honest seeker after truth, because already he is faced with God's general revelation and already he has an attitude against it. This attitude is real, though it may not be consciously thought through. It cannot be otherwise in God's world.

A missionary working in Borneo found an illustration of this in translation work. The translation of part of Romans had been prepared in draft and the first chapter was being read to a group in a traditional Bornean longhouse. The tribesfolk found the language quite understandable and were not unduly troubled by its complexity. One thing, however, concerned them : 'Yes, that is right,' they said, 'but how did he know how to write so accurately about our tribe?' Thus general revelation makes evangelism at once harder and easier. Harder, because we have to take the gospel to those who already have an attitude against God, as we once did. Easier, because they are God's creatures in His world; as such, the gospel has an ally and supporter in their conscience.

Now, however, we must return to the question of whether this distinction is one which the Bible supports.

Some roundly answer No. God is one, and His revelation is one. God reveals Himself through Christ and this revelation is unique and complete. In Christ God has revealed Him*self*, His one being. God cannot be known at one time as Creator and Judge apart from Christ, and then at another as Redeemer in Christ. This destroys the unity of God. To put up another revelation alongside Christ is to set up a rival to Him, and that is unthinkable. There is no alternative source of the knowledge of God; there is Christ only. It is through Him alone that we know of God as Creator as well as Redeemer.

Such a view is extremely plausible. It aims to give pre-eminence to Christ and so finds an echo in every Christian heart. Anything that competes with Christ's person or work must be rejected. But this is not a correct picture. In the first place it misrepresents the point of the distinction between general and saving revelation. Certainly Scripture attests the unity of God and forbids all thought of two rival revelations. But this has never been suggested. General revelation is not another revelation alongside saving truth, certainly not a secondary source of divine knowledge, and still less an attack on revelation in Christ. There are not two revelations, but simply two aspects of God's total self-disclosure.

In the second place, see what Scripture says. What we mean by general revelation comes out in such passages as these : 'The heavens are telling the glory of God; and the firmament proclaims his handiwork' (Ps. 19 : 1). 'He made from one every nation . . . that they should seek God . . .' (Acts 17 : 26, 27). 'For what can be known about God is plain to them . . . Ever since the creation of the world his invisible nature, namely, his eternal power and deity, has been clearly perceived in the things that have been made. So they are without excuse . . .' (Rom. 1 : 19, 20).

What kind of knowledge or revelation is implied here? Not one that can bring man to experience a saving relationship with God apart from Christ; that would constitute a 'natural theology' and Scripture has no place for any such view. It is a revelation linked directly with God's creative work; it speaks only of His eternal power, of the fact of the one God. It makes man responsible to God ('so they are without excuse'), but does not deal with his guiltiness. It leaves man culpable if he does not honour God as God or give thanks to Him (Rom. 1 : 21), but it does not offer the power to change man's heart.

It is thus, as G. C. Berkouwer said, a reminder of the guilt of closed eyes. 'Although they knew God . . . their senseless minds were darkened' (Rom. 1 : 21). Man must answer to God, but he cannot. Apart from any knowledge of Christ, man is accountable to God. God holds him guilty on the basis of the things that have been made, and which are there to be seen by all who have eyes. But man has not even lived up to the limited knowledge of God available to him.

All this prepares the way for God's saving revelation in Christ. In limited respects it is like the ministry of John the Baptist. John's was a restricted message : repentance. He was to make men aware of sin so that they would see the answer in Christ. John made ready for the Coming One who brought the saving message and said: 'Repent, *and* believe in the gospel' (Mk. 1 :15). There was a unity in the two messages (man's sin and the need of repentance) but there was also a distinction (one prepared, the other fulfilled). Similarly general revelation, though it does not tell of Christ, prepares the way for Him.

This brings us to look at special revelation. This is the complement of all that has emerged above about general revelation. It concerns Christ and leads to salvation. It brings a remedy where general revelation can only offer a diagnosis. It is gracious and life-giving. It makes men wise to salvation in Christ. It creates and strengthens faith, both as assent to truth and as trust in the living Saviour. To this we now turn.

CHAPTER THREE

GOD IN ACTION

IMAGINE THAT YOU had been present in Jerusalem
at the time of one of the many executions outside the city
wall. You have some acquaintance with the city and its
customs. You happen to pass the place where three men
are being crucified and gather that one of them is a bit of
a seven-day wonder. He is a wandering preacher, Jesus by
name, from Nazareth further north; according to some
rumours, he had political ambitions. And now he dies.

As you stood there, you would of course have witnessed
the death of Jesus. And what would you have made of it?
You might have recognized that event as one decisive for
all history. Conceivably you might have fallen down and
worshipped. You might even have grasped the genuine
reason for His death. Knowing what you *now* know, you
might have reacted thus. But without knowing from Scripture what was actually taking place, you would probably
not have understood it any more than did the majority of
onlookers. 'Just another set of crucifixions! We've seen it
all before. A bit more fuss about this one perhaps; but so
what?'

The death of Christ did not in fact make any wide-
spread impression at the time. This is surprising. After all,
Christ's cross is the greatest revelation of God's holiness
and grace, His justice and mercy. John wrote: 'In this
the love of God was made manifest among us, that God

sent his only Son into the world . . . to be the (propitiation) for our sins' (1 Jn. 4 :9, 10).

But the problem is this : how could any bystander in Jerusalem discern that this particular crucifixion (and no other) displayed such divine truths? Outwardly all crucifixions were pretty much the same. And if the observer recognized something divine in this death, how could he know *what* it revealed about God?

Pentecost presents the same difficulty. The crowd saw something unusual and tried to explain it. They gave it a naturalistic interpretation : 'they are filled with new wine' (Acts 2 :13). They were not to know the truth of the matter – that the Holy Spirit of God had come in all His shattering significance and supernatural power.

Or go back to one of the high points in Israel's history: the exodus. What was that event? To any secular chronicler it would have appeared as just another national migration, a people on the move from one country to another. Yet this particular exodus was a vehicle of divine revelation. It exhibited God's power, His grace, His covenant faithfulness, His judgments.

THE GOD WHO ACTS

Now this raises acute problems. Is God not active in all the movements of history? Why did not other deaths or other migrating peoples reveal Him? Is God not Lord of history after all? Yes, He is : this is the unanimous verdict of the Scripture writers : He works all things according to the counsel of His will (Eph. 1 : 11). Through Amos God reminded Israel : 'Did I not bring up Israel from the land of Egypt, and the Philistines from Caphtor and the Syrians from Kir?' (Am. 9 :7). Through Isaiah God said that He was bringing Assyria against His people, though the Assyrian 'does not so intend, and his mind does not so think' (Is. 10 :7).

Such passages stress that everything that happens is under God's control. When God brought the Israelites out of Egypt, they could begin to learn that this was so. But God's kingship was not merely over them, but over all – including the Philistines, the Syrians and the Assyrians. All history is in His hands.

But while God actuates all history, He discloses Himself only in some history. He discloses Himself in those acts that He intended to have a bearing on redemption. So He is rightly called the God who acts. Indeed the Old Testament itself draws the distinction between the living God who does whatever He pleases (Dn. 4 :35) and idols who cannot speak or walk, do good or evil (Je. 10 :5, 10).

How then do certain events reveal God? One answer is that which William Temple advocated when he wrote: 'There is no such thing as revealed truth . . . There are truths of revelation, that is to say, propositions which express the result of correct thinking concerning revelation; but they are not themselves directly revealed.'[1] Elsewhere he defined revelation as 'intercourse of mind and event, not the communication of doctrine distilled from that intercourse'. This suggests that revelation is uninterpreted divine action; men are left to reflect on and make their inferences from that action. But does this fit the case?

It does not in fact do so, and for one simple reason : it overlooks the fact that God's acts (regarded as mere acts) are in themselves 'opaque'. The events enable us to see that something has been going on, but in themselves they do not make its significance or meaning apparent. Bernard Ramm has likened this to looking at a television drama without the sound. Something is happening all right, but you can't make sense of it. J. I. Packer has caricatured it

[1] *Nature, Man and God*, p. 317.

as a 'divine charade to be solved by the God-inspired guess-work of the human spectators'.

This is the case with God's acts. Without these acts there would be no revelation, no salvation. Part of the uniqueness of Christianity is that it does not merely give a list of divine decrees or *fiats*. It is rooted in history, based squarely on event and fact. There is no escaping what God has *done*. But this is not the whole story, for 'unexplained activity is not revelation; it may only be darkness. It is the capricious godlings of heathendom who act suddenly and devastatingly, and leave men to guess their whim or desire.'[2] No; the glory of Christianity is that God has acted *and* spoken. He has given the events of the drama and its words. He has turned on the sound track.

How then was the exodus revelatory? 'Because Moses was there to interpret it. It is through the prophetic interpreter that history becomes revelation.'[3] It is significant that the Egyptians were involved in the same events as the Israelites in the period leading up to the exodus; but there is no suggestion that they regarded them as revelation. They were not given the revelatory word. 'So with the Babylonians, or for that matter the Persians, at the time of the return from the Exile. It is also worth asking why the wars of ancient Israel and not those of, say, modern African nations should be held to be revelational. The deeds by themselves are not revelation.'[4]

How was the cross revelatory? Because God moved the writers (Old Testament as well as New) to preach and record *His* interpretation of the cross. The gospel is not

[2] R. A. Cole, *The Gospel according to St Mark* (Tyndale New Testament Commentaries), p. 20.
[3] J. A. Motyer, 'Scripture and Tradition'; an essay in *The Church of England and the Methodist Church*, ed. J. I. Packer, p. 13.
[4] L. Morris, 'Biblical Authority and the Concept of Inerrancy', *The Churchman*, 81.1 (Spring 1967), p. 32.

simply that 'Christ died', for that would tell us nothing except the historical fact. God's good news is that 'Christ died for our sins . . .' 'Christ also died for sins once for all, the righteous for the unrighteous, that he might bring us to God . . .' (1 Cor. 15:3; 1 Pet. 3:18). The fact must be accompanied by the God-given interpretation: this and this alone is revelation.

This is why the saving facts have power. Paul felt constrained by the love of Christ – it moved him to tremendous effort for Christ. And it did so, he tells us, because he put a certain interpretation on a certain event: 'Because we are convinced that one has died for all . . .'; that is, because we put a certain interpretation on the death of Christ (2 Cor. 5:4). Remove this (God-given) understanding of the cross and you remove the constraint of Christ's love.[5]

And how was Pentecost revelatory? Not simply because they 'began to speak in other tongues' (Acts 2:4), but because Peter interpreted the event to them: 'This is what was spoken by the prophet Joel . . . "that I will pour out my Spirit" . . .' (2:16, 17).

ACTS AND WORDS

Event plus explanation; this is the pattern all through Scripture. So much is this so that at some points part at least of the interpretation preceded the event, as in the prophecies of Christ's coming and death.

All this means that history as written in the Bible is presented from a particular perspective. It is selective, choosing to record and explain only certain happenings out of many apparently similar ones. Even within Christ's life and ministry, Scripture chooses to narrate and expound only some of His deeds and words. This does not

[5] Cf. J. Denney, *The Death of Christ*, p. 83.

mean that it sits lightly to history, for the Bible always has prime regard for historical fact. But equally it never writes bare history, a mere chronicle. It records its selected acts and words in order to bring out of them the meaning God intended men to receive through them.

Thus Scripture sometimes treats as important what a secular historian would regard as trivial; elsewhere it treats as primary what others might regard as incidental (*e.g.* the history of some of the 'lesser' kings of Israel and Judah). It ignores some great historical characters and highlights some obscure ones (it bypasses Caesar and focuses on a carpenter of Nazareth – this in the heyday of the Roman Empire!). It may schematize history, as Matthew seems to have done with the genealogy of Christ; or condense it, as Luke did in the book of Acts. It may at times arrange topically rather than chronologically. It gives us four 'Gospels' when we might have expected just one. But it does all this consciously, because it is governed by one overriding consideration in its fact-recording: it aims to bring out of all history only certain history; and so to present and explain *that* history as most clearly to reveal God.

CHAPTER FOUR

GOD SPEAKING

IN THE LAST CHAPTER we tried to show that God is not only 'the God who acts'. Revelation in history cries out for an accompanying revelation in word. The question is : has God in fact spoken? Is there such a thing as 'propositional' revelation?

Now clearly the Bible is not presented to us in the form of a schematized series of doctrinal propositions. Equally it is not in the form of a catechism of Christian doctrine, with neatly arranged questions and answers. It is a book with as much narrative as direct instruction and with a rich variety of literary forms. So the precise problem we have to face is this : granted the fact of God's actions, has He also revealed truth? Has He communicated knowledge, interpretation of fact, concepts – even information and propositions?

Some flatly deny this. Emil Brunner said : 'The Holy Scriptures do not teach theological doctrine.'[1] William Temple thought that we cannot take all the assertions of Scripture as revealed truth. Indeed, he asserted concerning the Bible as a whole : 'No single sentence can be quoted as having the authority of a distinct utterance of the All-Holy God.'[2] C. H. Dodd wrote that Jesus 'seems to have made very few general theological propositions, and those of the simplest'; and that 'the Bible's place as a

---

[1] *Reason and Revelation*, p. 149.
[2] *Nature, Man and God*, p. 350.

whole is rather with the masterpieces of poetry, drama and philosophy, that is, the literature which does not so much impart information but stirs the deeper levels of personality.'[3] In similar vein, G. E. Wright wrote: 'No system of propositions can deal adequately with the inner dynamics of Biblical faith.'[4]

Such views oppose any notion of conceptual, let alone verbal revelation. Revelation in history and act is one thing; but the idea of revelation in word is quite another. The first consists of hard, objective, unquestionable facts (though, ironically, many protagonists of this view then go on to question the facts); the second concerns 'soft', subjective, speculative ideas. Event is divine and absolute; word is human and relative. The one firm as rock; the other shifting as sand. And we all know where the wise man built his house . . . But can such a distinction be supported?

WORD AS EVENT

It is not going too far to suggest that words and actions are both events. As the saying goes, 'the pen is mightier than the sword'. Mere slogans ('Workers of the world, unite!') have had as great an impact on the destinies of men as physical happenings, wars and bombs. The rupture alleged between the acts recorded in Scripture (which reveal God) and the words there (which are human reflection) is more apparent than real.

It is the divine word which creates history. It is God's word to and through Elijah that creates a totally changed situation for Ahab, Jezebel and the prophets of Baal. God *told* Ahab that there would be no rain, except by His word (1 Ki. 17:1). Then 'the word of the Lord came' to

[3] *The Authority of the Bible*, pp. 265, 270.
[4] *God Who Acts*, p. 36.

Elijah, 'Depart . . .' (17:2); God's word withdrew Elijah from Ahab, leaving him without any way of knowing God's will. Then 'the word of the Lord came to Elijah, in the third year, saying, "Go, show yourself to Ahab . . ."' (18:1). Thus God's word created the situation for the contest on Mount Carmel with the 450 prophets of Baal. God's word caused Ahab to gather the people for this. God's word was itself an event, *the* event that counted.

This fact is heavily underlined by the importance that was attached to 'the word' in the Ancient Near East. In that world the 'word' was no mere vehicle of meaning. To the Hebrews it was something packed with power, something living, something real. It came, it worked, it transformed; it had a built-in impact adhesive for the situation. And it was never (let it be emphasized) separated in their minds from the one who spoke it.

This stands out in a passage such as Isaiah 9:8–12: 'The Lord has sent a word against Jacob, and it will light upon Israel; and all the people will know . . . So the Lord raises adversaries against them, and stirs up their enemies.' God sends His word as a king might send an army; indeed by a word God stirs up an army with drastic results : 'so the Lord cut off from Israel head and tail'. What could be more decisive? 'There are in fact some situations in which the deeds are almost non-existent, but where it is impossible to deny the revelation. A good example is the making of the covenant between God and His people on Sinai (Ex. 24). What did God actually *do* on this occasion? It is difficult to see any objective deed at all. But the revelation that at that time God had entered into coven- ant relationships with Israel was of profound importance for all the subsequent history of the nation.'[5] God's word establishing the covenant directed all their subsequent history.

[5] L. Morris, *op. cit.*

On reflection, we are not total strangers to this concept in our world today. Take a trivial example : look at two young children at play – the boy with his cars, the girl at her drawing. At one moment all is peace and harmony. Then the boy says : 'You've drawn a silly picture.' He only says it; he has done nothing. Yet her morning is ruined, her fun spoilt – by the mere words of a boy !

The power of the word is seen most clearly in the use of the phrase 'the word of the Lord'. This came to the prophets, gave them their message, put moral fibre into them, nerved their feeble arm for fight, and set them on their feet against kings and despots; the word of the Lord overturned the history that men thought they were writing. If you doubt this, take a concordance and check what happened in different contexts when God's word 'came'.

'By the word of the Lord the heavens were made, and all their host by the breath of his mouth' (Ps. 33 :6). 'And God said, "Let there be . . ." and it was so' (Gn. 1). God merely said. This same principle is dramatically seen in the life of Jesus. Take some incidents at random and observe how in each case He took a situation that was beyond hope and by His word alone brought about what was impossible :

The paralytic : Jesus *said* to the paralytic, 'Rise, take up your bed and go home.' 'And *he rose* and went home' (Mt. 9 :6, 7).

The man with the withered hand : 'He *said* to the man, "Stretch out your hand." And *the man stretched it out*, and it was restored, whole like the other' (Mt. 12 : 13).

The storm on the lake : 'And he awoke and *rebuked* the wind, and *said* to the sea, "Peace ! Be still !" And the wind *ceased*, and there was a great calm. . . . "Who then is this, that even wind and sea *obey* him?"' (Mk. 4 :39, 41).

Lazarus : Jesus *'cried* with a loud voice, "Lazarus,

come out." The *dead man came out* . . .' (Jn. 11:43, 44).

Notice that there was no outward, physical action, even of a symbolic nature. Christ simply spoke: His power and His word went together. No wonder that men stood in awe when the incarnate Lord of glory spoke with such authority and power. Thus Scripture affirms that 'the word of God is living and active, sharper than any two-edged sword . . .' (Heb. 4:12). The arrival of God's word means the presence of His power; it is an event more than capable of upsetting the *status quo*. Its coming is as dynamic as the coming of God Himself, for the One who speaks is inseparable from what He speaks.

The grounds therefore for making a radical disjunction between act and word in revelation are, to say the least, insecure. Revelation does not consist of acts alone; it has a valid conceptual and verbal aspect. Without this it is not revelation at all.

WORD AS PERSONAL

It is this very fact that makes it possible for individuals to know God personally.

Some have objected to propositional revelation on the very ground that it works against personal encounter with God. Such revelation, they say, leads merely to an intellectual assent to statements and inevitably falls short of personal confrontation and commitment. It touches only one part of man – his mind. Revelation viewed as encounter, on the other hand, affects the whole man – mind, will, affections, conscience—and embraces him in a living relationship with the living God. Faith, on this understanding, arises out of meeting Him, not from hearing information about Him.

Such an argument appeals strongly to all who value personal trust in Christ. But it is an argument falsely based. To be valid, it must assume that revelation in word means merely a disclosure of information, of abstract theological or philosophical assertions. But who ever said that propositional revelation meant that abstractions were the purest form of divine revelation? Certainly not those who believe in propositional revelation. Bernard Ramm has put the situation picturesquely: 'The statement, "God's omniscience and omnipotence secure the providential care of my life", does not quite reproduce, "The Lord is my shepherd, I shall not want".'[6] The plain fact is that God chose to give us these truths in the personal form of Psalm 23. But the point is that the Psalm does give us propositions. The knowledge that Psalm 23 (as a typical case) imparts is emphatically intellectual; that is, it comes to us through our minds. But with equal emphasis we must say that such knowledge is not intellectualistic; it is knowledge of *His* grace and *His* care, and evokes our trust and the response of our whole being.

So it is specious to imagine that revelation is disclosure of a person but not of truth. After all, how do people come to know each other? What happens when two people fall in love? They meet, as often as possible, and spend time together. But this is not all; every instinct within them cries out for them to declare their love to each other. Words, of course, can be empty symbols; they can even be blatant lies. Yet friendship, love and commitment without words is scarcely conceivable. Words impart mutual knowledge. This is why, when lovers are apart from each other, they sometimes value a letter even more than a present. Why? Because a letter reveals more and tells them how much they are missed. Obviously, if no present were ever given, doubt could be cast on the sincerity of the words. But the *words* 'I love you' have an essential and dynamic part in creating and cementing the relationship.

[6] *Special Revelation and the Word of God*, p. 39.

As it stands, 'I love you' is a bare proposition, abstract, cold. Conceivably, if no personal encounter were taking place, it could be received in that way. But within a true personal relationship, such propositions are not unwelcome intruders but vital and integral to those concerned.

There is a significant little incident concerning the Israelites as they were about to enter Canaan. The only written revelation they had then was 'this law'. By comparison with what we have in the Pentateuch (let alone in the Old Testament or in the whole Bible) it was the merest scrap of revelation. If ever a situation was designed for people to seek immediate revelation or direct encounter, this was it. Yet they were simply commanded to assemble regularly to '*hear* and learn to fear the Lord . . . and be careful to do all the words of this law' (Dt. 31 :9–13). Even when most could not read, they were not to dispense with what was written.

We shall look later at the manner in which propositions are set out in the Bible. But we may say now, on the basis of what we have seen, that they are in no way anti-personal, anti-encounter or merely academic; rather, the exact opposite. If God simply encounters a person, demanding (as one writer has put it) 'decision, obedience and passion', how is that person to know for whom or what he is to decide, to whom or what he is to yield his obedience, about whom he is to be passionate? This is no side issue, to be left in the 'pending' tray of the professional theologian. It is crucial for experimental Christianity.

The apostle Paul is a vivid illustration of this. He had the most dramatic encounter with the risen Christ on the road to Damascus. His whole life was transformed : from 'breathing threats and murder against the disciples of the Lord' (Acts 9 :1) he became the man who could say, 'the love of Christ controls us' (2 Cor. 5 :14). What made this revolution in him? According to some, he would have replied, 'My encounter on the Damascus road, where Christ met me and demanded my decision, obedience and passion'. Surely Paul is the classic example of one who was transformed by encounter, not propositions. Now we do not undervalue the tremendous thing that God did in and to Paul at that moment; Scripture itself attaches the highest significance in the life of the individual to new birth, leading to repentance and faith. But the significant thing is that Paul does not give this answer. He does not put his about-turn down merely to encounter. When he said before Agrippa that he 'was not disobedient to the heavenly vision' (Acts 26:19), he goes on to show that this meant precise obedience to what the Lord had *said* to him. He sought to obey to the letter the terms (that is, the words) of his commission from Christ. As we saw in the last chapter, it was his Lord's understanding of His death that put Paul in the grip of His love.

To Paul, 'God was in Christ reconciling the world to himself' (2 Cor. 5:19) was a proposition; but it did not destroy or intellectualize Paul's devotion to God. It did not give him just another item of brain-fodder; it shaped and warmed his gratitude to Christ. It enabled him to affirm : the Son of God 'loved me and gave himself for me' (Gal. 2:20).

To rule out conceptual, propositional, verbal revelation is to deny to God omnipotent one of the essential features of personhood. It is to make Him less than man and so to hinder personal encounter, if not to prevent it altogether. It is to relegate the words of prophets, apostles and even the Lord Christ Himself from the category of revealed truths (by which God in person speaks) to that of human reflection (however exalted). Without the communication of truth, God becomes a mere force and faith becomes mysticism.

This can have the most serious consequences for Christian living and obedience. In the Bible faith is always trust in God and in what He has *said*. This is the central thrust of Hebrews 11 : 'By faith Noah, being warned by God . . . took heed . . .' (verse 7). 'By faith Abraham obeyed when he was called . . .' (verse 8). 'By faith' Moses 'left Egypt . . . kept the Passover . . .' (verses 28, 29). Remove God's word from the experiences of these men and their faith becomes unreason, wishful thinking, delusion. But God's word, both as command and promise, gives their faith its unshakable foundation. And thus they are an example to us, since we are called to live by faith in God in this same sense – of giving full response to what God says.

CHAPTER FIVE

HOW HAS GOD SPOKEN?

HOW CAN HUMAN LANGUAGE convey God's voice? All such language has built-in limitations. Even when words are translated from one human language to another, it is impossible always to convey every shade of meaning in the original. How much harder for divine meaning to be enshrined accurately in symbols for men. Surely language will inevitably distort the divine truth it seeks to convey?

To some this is an end of argument; God's eternal truth cannot possibly be reflected accurately via human language.

At least two answers may be made to this. The first concerns *the nature and function of language*. 'Language, we may say, extracts from our fleeting temporal experience certain recurrent themes.'[1] Its function is to preserve and convey meaning, and so provide a framework for thought. It draws out the meaning of past experiences and in that way carries a present meaning to us. Take the word 'recreation' for example. Because it recalls specific past activities it conveys sense to me now; because of this it helps me to anticipate future ones. The word brings the meaning to mind and so aids clarity of thought. Thus, while our human experience is limited, there is no reason why God should not extract, by the use of symbols He sees to be appropriate, those themes which can speak truly of Him.

[1] Harry Blamires, *A Defence of Dogmatism*, p. 78.

The second concerns *man's ability to form symbols* and imbue them with significance. Man acquired this power because God gave it to him; it stems from the fact that he was made in the image of God. Genesis 2 :19–23 implies this: 'Whatever the man called every living creature, that was its name . . . Then the man said, "This at last is bone of my bones and flesh of my flesh; she shall be called Woman" . . .' Thus, although language (as every lover knows) has limitations, there is no *a priori* reason why it should not be the bearer of divine news. The language of finite men may not be adequate to carry an exhaustive knowledge of the inexhaustible glory of God's being; but this does not mean that it cannot transmit true knowledge.

God's revelation is made 'to accommodate the knowledge of God to our feebleness',[2] to mediate God to us, rather than to communicate an unmediated awareness of Him. In a parallel way, the disciples did not see 'the Word in the beginning with God', but 'the Word made flesh'. They saw and knew the Word who 'dwelt among us, full of grace and truth; we have beheld his glory . . .' (Jn. 1 :1,14); but they did not behold Him in His unmasked, pre-incarnate glory. They had what F. A. Schaeffer calls 'true truth', though they did not have exhaustive knowledge.[3]

FORMS AND LANGUAGE

What then does this mean about special revelation through language? Three points may be brought out here. First, that *special revelation is marked throughout by human characteristics*. Take a few examples :

(a) *God is described as having bodily parts:* 'The

---

[2] John Calvin, *Institutes of the Christian Religion*, I, XIII, 1.
[3] *Escape from Reason*, p. 21.

magicians said to Pharaoh, "This is the *finger* of God"'
(Ex. 8 :19, *cf.* our Lord in Lk. 11 :20). 'Man lives by everything that proceeds out of the *mouth* of the Lord' (Dt.
8 :3). 'Behold, the *eye* of the Lord is on those who fear
him' (Ps. 33 :18). 'My *hand* laid the foundation of the
earth' (Is. 48 :13). And so on.

(b) *He is described in terms of man's mental activity:*
'For my *thoughts* are not your thoughts . . .' (Is. 55 :8).

(c) *Human emotions are even ascribed to Him.* 'Has he
in *anger* shut up his *compassion*?' (Ps. 77 :9). 'He will not
always chide, nor will he keep his *anger* for ever . . . As a
father *pities* his children, so the Lord pities those who
fear him' (Ps. 103 :9,13).

Such anthropomorphisms are not incidental, but occur
throughout the Bible. At first sight they seem to be merely
man's fallible attempts to imagine God, to snatch at ideas
quite beyond his reach. They appear to give us a 'god'
who is merely a projection of man's confined notions.
Such is the view of some who deny revelation in word.
But if God has been pleased to reveal Himself through
human language, then these are exactly the symbols by
which He has opted to picture Himself to us. The particular human characteristics of Scripture language were
selected by God for this purpose.

This leads us to the second point : *special revelation is
marked by the use of analogy.* Take the expression 'the
eye of God'. Our eyes make us aware of what is going on
around us. So God conveys to us His total awareness of all
that goes on in His world by this analogy. The phrase 'the
eye of God' is not a perfect representation of God's being,
since God as spirit has no bodily parts; nevertheless the
phrase is understandable and is accurate to convey the
sense intended. This means that God has taken those features of our finite life which He sees can convey by
analogy particular aspects of His person or work. We

cannot presume that any analogy which we can conjure up will enshrine truth about God, for the authenticity of the analogies in Scripture is that God Himself has drawn them for us. The end result of this revelation through analogy is to give a knowledge of God which finite sinners of every age may comprehend.

In the third place, *special revelation involves different modes and forms*. In summary we may distinguish three here. Farthest back in time was the era of *external signs* : theophanies, visible symbols and physical phenomena such as the burning bush and the cloudy pillar. These were mainly in the time of the patriarchs. Then in the age of the prophets God frequently spoke by *inward suggestion* : the phrase 'the word of the Lord came to me' does not specify whether any voice was heard, yet the prophet knew that it was God speaking nonetheless. Finally came what B. B. Warfield called *concursive operation*. Revelation in this form meant that no human activities were superseded, but the Holy Spirit worked in, with and through them all to achieve His object. The prophet or apostle, that is, might speak or write without any particular consciousness of 'being inspired'; their words were thus consciously human, yet also fully divine.

These forms were not rigidly confined within these historical periods, and it is impossible to put them into watertight compartments. We are not suggesting that these were the only forms of special revelation through language, for there were also such modes as dreams and visions. These are mentioned just as illustrations of the fact that God gave His self-disclosure in complementary ways. No form is presented as inferior, for all alike under the providence of God convey true knowledge of Him. 'In many and various ways God spoke of old to our fathers by the prophets; but in these last days he has spoken to us by a Son' (Heb. 1 : 1).

CHAPTER SIX

IS THE BIBLE GOD'S VOICE?

GOD HAS ACTED in human history; God has spoken through human language. The great question is : what connection is there between this revelation and the Bible? The view of the church down the years, as set out in the many confessions of faith, has been that there is the most intimate connection : the Bible *is* the Word of God. Much more recently, however, some have asserted a clear distinction between the 'Word of God' on the one hand and the Bible on the other. The Word of God may be within the Bible, but cannot be identified with it. 'The doctrine of the verbal inspiration of Holy Scripture . . . cannot be regarded as an adequate formulation of the authority of the Bible. It is a product of the views of late Judaism, not of Christianity.'[1]

This distinction is of immense practical consequence for personal and public use of the Bible. If the Bible is the Word of God, you may expect to hear God Himself speaking to your profit in every part of Scripture. At the lowest estimate, Scripture is always worth reading. By contrast, if the Bible merely contains the Word of God, you have to determine somehow whether the passage you are reading is or is not His Word. Or if it may become His Word (but is not that as it stands), you have a problem if on any given day it does not seem to 'become'. Even if it seems to become, you have to distinguish God's voice from your

[1] Emil Brunner, *Reason and Revelation*, pp. 127, 128.

emotions. The same applies to the public use of the Bible :
on this view there is no reason why anyone, in pulpit or
Bible study group or Sunday school, should consistently
teach or proclaim what Scripture says.

What then is the truth of the matter? Is revelation one
thing, its embodiment in a book quite another? The issue
we must take up is this : where should we start our study
of inspiration?

TWO APPROACHES

Two approaches have their advocates. Some say that the
proper procedure is to start with the phenomena of Scripture and make your inferences about inspiration from
them. This is the *inductive* method. Others take the *deductive* approach : the clear statements in Scripture about
its own nature are primary; you must make your deduc-
tions from those.

According to the first, we must not start with any preconceived notions about the Bible, but piece our view
together from studying the relevant passages and factors.
Taking the Gospels, for example, we must look at the
various accounts of any one incident or saying and construct our doctrine of inspiration on that evidence. We
must scrutinize parallel accounts in Old Testament narratives, ponder the New Testament's use of the Old and
examine all apparent discrepancies.

There is real plausibility in this approach : do not just
pick out isolated assertions, it says, look at the Bible as a
whole. But does this procedure in fact do that? Does it
look at all the facts? To begin by looking at the phenomena (as distinct from the assertions) implies that, at
least at the outset, I set aside the direct statements in
which Scripture describes itself. So my approach is partial, not whole after all. Initially I have to exclude the

clear pronouncements in order to be in a position to look without bias at the 'facts'. I therefore tend to pit the claims against the phenomena. But the Bible does make claims about itself, it does give us teaching about its origin and nature; these are themselves part of the phenomena. If these statements are in fact God's own description of the Bible, must they not determine my initial approach? Nothing can warrant setting God's own affirmations in a secondary place. Certainly, induction from the observed facts of the Bible will have its essential place; it may well bring me to adjust certain misunderstandings to which the deductive process on its own might lead me. But I am free to see and study the book as a whole only when I take God's statements about it as primary. In this way these claims link up and fit in with the phenomena.

Take a limited but not irrelevant analogy. Imagine someone coming now to examine the person of Christ. He is faced with two related factors : the observed life of Christ on the one hand – where He went, what He did, what aroused His compassion or anger. On the other, he reads the definite claims which the Lord made about Himself. Now of course, Christ stands before us as one complete person (just as the Bible faces us as one unified book), so that the deeds and the sayings are inextricably woven together. But in practice the observer has to start at some point; which set of facts comes first? This was the dilemma which faced the Jewish people and leaders in the lifetime of Jesus. This was their attitude : rejecting Christ's self-testimony, they started with the remaining 'facts'. On this basis, they found that Christ was at variance at almost every point with *their* preconceived view of the Old Testament and religion in general. No wonder that they could not begin to make sense of Him, for their error was in starting with the 'facts' and not re-garding Christ's own claims as primary. Christ was not crucified for His good life, but because He had 'made himself the Son of God' (Jn. 19 : 7).

So we must begin with Christ's self-testimony and Scripture's self-testimony. This gives us the indispensable vantage point from which to survey the phenomena. And from that perspective the facts are found to support and fill out the claims. My purpose here therefore is to begin with the material in the Bible which sets out its own understanding of itself. Then I shall examine and try to answer some of the objections to this view.

WHAT CONFIRMS THE NEW TESTAMENT?

To arrive at a right view of any truth, we must remember that Scripture is a book of examples and illustrations as well as straightforward statements. It conveys its teaching both by formal assertions and incidental allusions. To arrive at a right view of this particular doctrine of inspiration, we need to recall that, in the nature of the case, most of the references will be in the New Testament about the Old. This is reflected in our quotations below, and raises a problem. If the New Testament confirms the inspiration of the Old, what confirms that of the New? There is no Third Testament. In fact three lines of evidence converge to help us here.

First, *the fact and nature of apostleship*. This is relevant because the New Testament books were written by apostles or those intimately associated with them. The mere fact that apostles had seen the risen Christ did not alone make them unique. What did distinguish them was the fact that they had received a revelation of Christ that was in no sense mediated through men. Our knowledge of Christ comes through the Scripture writers, but the apostles' came direct from God. Paul rubbed this point home to the Galatians : 'Paul an apostle – not from men

nor through man, but through Jesus Christ and God the
Father ... When he was pleased to reveal his Son in me ...
I did not confer with flesh and blood, nor did I go up to
Jerusalem to those who were apostles before me, but I
went away' (1:1,16,17). Thus the writers of the New
Testament had received revelation from God in quite as
direct a way as their Old Testament counterparts.

Second, *the relevant allusions within the New Testament*. Peter puts Paul's writings on a par with 'the other
scriptures' (2 Pet. 3:16). Paul claimed (as an apostle) to
speak and write 'in words not taught by human wisdom
but taught by the Spirit' and thus to 'have the mind of
Christ' (1 Cor. 2:13,16). Elsewhere Paul treats passages
from Old and New Testaments as equally Scripture.
From Deuteronomy 25:4 he quotes, 'You shall not muzzle
an ox when it is treading out the grain.' From our Lord's
own words recorded in Matthew 10:10 and Luke 10:7
he quotes, 'The labourer deserves his wages'. Significantly
he introduces both with the single formula : 'for the scripture says' (1 Tim. 5:18). Nor is that all. In 1 Corinthians
9:9 he again cites Deuteronomy 25:4; five verses later he
brings out its application by referring to the fact that 'the
Lord commanded that those who proclaim the gospel
should get their living by the gospel' (1 Cor. 9:14). An
Old Testament reference, a New Testament reference and
a saying of Jesus were, to Paul, equally God's word.

Third, *Christ's own teaching*. The claims made by New
Testament writers follow naturally out of Christ's promise
to the disciples concerning the Holy Spirit : 'He will take
what is mine and declare it to you' (Jn. 16:14). The Spirit
was to take the things that they could not bear then and
reveal them to the disciples. This is more than the Spirit's
ordinary work of illuminating individual minds to see
truth already revealed. This is the Spirit revealing new
truth to the apostles or those closely associated with them.

We shall see what this implies about oral tradition later, but the most obvious reference of this is to the production of the New Testament.

Quite apart from such references, however, it is plain fact that the Old Testament seems harder to accept than the New. If we find that Christ accepted the Old, with all its apparent problems, as the Word of God, there will be relatively little difficulty in so accepting the New. Few, having swallowed the camels, will strain at the gnats.

What then is the meaning of inspiration? The direct teaching, incidental allusions and observed facts of Scripture point to its having two main aspects, *divine* and *human*.

THE DIVINE ORIGIN OF THE BIBLE

Let us take some of the most obvious direct statements of the Bible about this:

'*All scripture is inspired by God*' (2 Tim. 3:16). Paul is writing primarily about the nature of Scripture here, although this has been partially obscured by contrasting translations of the verse. Some versions have rendered it as 'all scripture is inspired of God and profitable' (RSV, AV); others have taken it as 'every inspired scripture is profitable' (RV, NEB). From one angle this is not a vast difference. 'All scripture' clearly presents Paul's conviction that his Bible is inspired all through. 'Every scripture' would mean that Paul was thinking of Scripture's many different parts (the law, the prophets and the writings) or books and taking each as inspired. The one considers Scripture as a unit; the other envisages its component parts.

Some, however, have inferred from 'every inspired scripture is profitable' that Paul thought that some parts of Scripture were neither inspired nor profitable. This is not an inference Paul would have entertained. His use of quotations from the Old Testament offers no support to this idea. Indeed there is no shred of evidence from the rest of his writings that Paul had any doubt about the divine origin of the whole Old Testament. All the evidence is that he regarded it as his Lord had done before him. If a view of partial inspiration had not been adopted already on other grounds, it is hard to see how it could have been found in this verse, let alone on other evidence. It is fair to conclude that the AV and RSV give the more natural reading of the original.

We must return to the main thrust of the verse to ask what Paul is conveying about the nature of Scripture. 'Inspired by God' (*theopneustos*) does not teach what Scripture does but rather what it is. What it does actively comes next, when Paul speaks of Scripture as being profitable to equip us for every good work. In *theopneustos* he is affirming the nature of the Bible : it is 'breathed out by God'. His meaning is not obscure. When people speak they breathe out words. We refer to some politicians (and preachers) as 'talking a lot of hot air'. At least our slang conveys the notion of breath producing and bearing words. On a quite different level, yet in a not dissimilar way, Paul says that God breathed out or produced Scripture. Its origin is in Him. It is His product, through His breath, His spirit. God's revealing activity did not end when chosen individuals received His Word. It continued, to ensure that His breathed-out word was written down and preserved.

'*Men moved by the Holy Spirit spoke from God*' (2 Pet. 1 :21). In this passage Peter is thinking ahead to the situation his readers will face when he is dead. When he as an apostle is no longer able to teach them, they will need to know what to take as the basis for their faith. So he reminds them of three factors :

(a) *Negatively*, they can rest assured that they have not followed cleverly devised myths.

(b) *Positively*, they have followed what was authentic because it was apostolic. They believed those who had actually heard the Father's testimony to His Son. (This ties up with what we have already said about apostolic testimony being authentic because it was direct from God and not mediated through men. *Cf.* Gal. 1 : 1, 15, 17.)

(c) *Additionally* they have the 'prophetic word'. This sounds a rather vague phrase, but in fact his readers could scarcely have understood it except as a reference to the Old Testament. That Testament is the only 'word' which fits Peter's threefold description : *first*, it was already in existence, and sufficiently familiar to them to need only a passing reference to bring it to mind. *Second*, it was a word to which they would still be able to pay attention after Peter's death. *Third*, it possessed a prophetic, thus-says-the-Lord quality and did not originate in any human initiative.

The men through whom this came were 'carried along' by the Spirit to His desired destination. The same verb is used in Acts 27 : 15, 17 of the ship on which Paul was sailing to Rome : 'and when the ship was caught and could not face the wind, we gave way to it and were *driven*.' The Holy Spirit bore men along so that it was His divine power that determined what they spoke and wrote, not 'the impulse of man'.

AS ORIGINALLY GIVEN

Before we proceed, one question arises at this point : to what were Paul and Peter referring in these assertions? Surely it was to Scripture as produced by God. It is difficult to see to what else their statements could possibly apply except to Scripture as originally given. They were not talking about manuscript copying or translation, which necessary processes are not totally exempt from human frailty.

This does not mean that these latter processes were at the mercy of fortune. Copying of these ancient documents was undertaken with meticulous care and checking. The manuscripts themselves, being regarded as of divine origin, were copied with a correspondingly high sense of responsibility. God has undoubtedly kept His Word from being obscured in transmission down the centuries. That does not alter the fact that inspiration refers to the writing, not the subsequent copying and translation, of the Bible.

Referring to what was thus written (the *graphē*), Bernard Ramm points out the significance of this : 'Because no translation is a perfect reproduction of the *graphē* in its original languages, the Christian Church can never grant any version the same status it does the *graphē* in its original Hebrew, Aramaic and Greek. The Christian Church must teach at the same time that the *graphē* can be adequately translated into other languages and so be an authentic product of special revelation, but that no such translation can ever have the same status as the *graphē* in its original languages.'[2]

Of course, we do not have the autograph manuscripts. But does this make these facts irrelevant? Not at all, and for at least four reasons :

First, because we must in all honesty give some answer to the question of what 'inspiration' refers to; if it is not to Scripture as God gave it in its different parts at different times, to what can it relate? Some edition of the original? Some translation?

[2] *Special Revelation and the Word of God*, p. 200.

Second, because 'by the "singular care and providence" of God the Bible text has come down to us in such substantial purity that even the most uncritical edition of the Hebrew and Greek, or the most incompetent or even the most tendentious translation of such an edition, cannot effectively obscure the real message of the Bible, or neutralize its saving power.'[3]

Third, because this is the continual incentive both to textual research and study and to translation work. For instance, a missionary may be translating the Bible for an Indian tribe in South America. Something may be lost in his translation (the nearest tribal word may say less than the Greek); equally something may be added (the tribal culture may introduce new associations with certain words). Now the missionary could be content just to pass on some general truths about God, without fretting about their exact expression. In fact he takes great pains to find the most appropriate individual words and phrases. Why? Because he is anxious to give to the tribe the nearest rendering he can find to the sense (and therefore the wording) of the original. 'As originally given' has a most practical relevance for him.

And fourth, because the truthfulness of God Himself is at stake in this. Are we to believe that God did not give a pure text at each point? 'Upon receiving a letter filled with trifling errors and mis-spelled words, we are displeased and annoyed; the letter casts reflection upon its writer ... The Scriptures claim to be breathed forth from His mouth; if they partake of error, must He not Himself partake thereof?'[4]

---

[3] F. F. Bruce, 'As Originally Given', *A Symposium from Past Terminal Letters* of the Theological Students' Fellowship, pp. 7, 8.
[4] E. J. Young, *Thy Word is Truth*, pp. 86, 87.

IS THE BIBLE GOD'S VOICE?

JESUS' ATTITUDE TO SCRIPTURE

To return to the Bible's propositions about itself, what are our Lord's own views? We may take some typical examples :

(a) John 10 :34f. brings us Christ's defence against the Pharisees; it was no occasion for trivial arguments, for they would have stoned Him for blasphemy. His defence was an appeal to the Scriptures. He quotes in fact from Psalm 82 :6 by asking, 'Is it not written in your *law* . . .?' Now the Psalms were not technically part of the law; they could only be called such if the entire Old Testament was God's law and shared His indefectible authority. In this sense He said 'the Scripture cannot be broken'. Scripture stands; as law it is always binding. And it is precisely because it is God's law, the Word of God, that it is right and worthwhile for Christ to appeal to it.

It is scarcely likely that Christ picked on the one verse in the Psalter which was 'law', or the one inspired part in the Old Testament. Rather His use of an ordinary part of the canon in this way suggests that He regarded it as being God's word, even down to its most casual parts and their form of expression.

(b) Mark 12 :10 shows Christ wondering at how the chief priests, scribes and elders could read the Old Testament with such total lack of understanding. 'Have you not read this scripture . . .?' He said, implying that, had they done so, they would have found divine truth about Him. As He said later to the Sadducees (Mk. 12 :24), the source of all error in the things of God (and especially concerning Himself) was ignorance of the Scriptures : 'Is not this why you are wrong, that you know neither the scriptures nor the power of God?' (This verse is interesting also in that it shows that to Christ 'the scriptures' and 'the power of God' were linked concepts. He did not sub-scribe to the view that what was written was a dead letter.) To Him Scripture was utterly true because it was from God.

(c) Matthew 19:4f. records Christ quoting Genesis 2:24. The Pharisees tested Him by asking, 'Is it lawful to divorce one's wife for any cause?' He answered, 'Have you not read that he who made them from the beginning made them male and female, and said, "For this reason a man shall leave his father and mother..."?' What Christ quotes is simply part of the Genesis narrative and is not intro-duced by 'and God said...' This is the Creator's saying only if all Scripture is. What therefore is written is the Word of God.

(d) The above references show Christ appealing to the Old Testament in teaching or debate with others. Mat-thew 4:1–11 indicates that He viewed the book in the same way when He was alone. In His temptation, when there was no possibility of accommodation or *argumen-tum ad hominem*, what Scripture said settled His personal conduct. Why was 'it is written' final for Him? Because it was His Father's voice. To say that authority in Christ's life resided in His own consciousness *or* in His Father's will *or* in Scripture is, in the last analysis, to say the same thing. His consciousness was governed by His Father's will which was expressed in Scripture. There was no con-tradiction between them; they were one.

Such references to Scripture can hardly have been placed in Christ's mouth. They are too constant, too in-tegral, too minute, too incidental, too pervasive of all the channels of His teaching.

Thus Scripture is, in all its parts, divine due to its origin in God who 'breathed it out'.

IS THE BIBLE GOD'S VOICE?

THE HUMAN ASPECTS OF THE BIBLE

Scripture came into being through the instrumentality of men. This is well illustrated in Mark 12 :36 and Acts 1 :16 : 'David himself, inspired by the Holy Spirit, declared . . .' and 'the Holy Spirit spoke beforehand by the mouth of David . . .' It is a fact of great consequence that Scripture is attributed (as in these examples) to both God and man, and to either God or man. This signifies co-authorship, through the divine origin and the human instruments. The whole of Scripture is from God; equally the whole of it is through men. It is not that some parts are divine and other parts human; all of it shares both characteristics. We can now examine the human features more fully.

These are so obvious as scarcely to need enumerating. Each writer has his own style, his own vocabulary and turns of phrase. Paul could hardly be mistaken for John; Isaiah would not readily be confused with the writer of Proverbs. Each writer employs particular literary forms; each writes in and out of his own background. Even in treating the same basic material as in the Gospels, the writers do not veil their individual approach; this is distinctive to them personally, while they are each complementary to the other.

All this is evidence of the humanity of the book. Anything less calculated to form a basis for a theory of dictation as the mode of inspiration is hard to conceive. Indeed, this evidence of the genuine humanness of Scripture demonstrates the providence of God in preparing the writers. God was not reduced to scanning the world from heaven in order to pick the best of a poor lot as His penmen. Rather He prepared His chosen men for this work in the most thorough way. Intending to use Paul, He (as Paul wrote in Gal. 1 :15) 'set me apart before I was born' and 'was pleased to reveal his Son in me, in order that I might preach him . . .' (1 :16). Paul's parents, ancestry, religious education, experiences, thought-forms and temperament were all under God's guiding hand. When in due time Paul came to write freely and spontaneously he was exactly the person God purposed him to be to perform his particular role.

This applies, of course, to the other writers of Scripture, and some make explicit mention of it. Jeremiah wrote of his appointment as prophet and to account for it he referred to what God had said : 'Before I formed you in the womb I knew you, and before you were born I consecrated you; I appointed you a prophet to the nations . . . Behold, I have put my words in your mouth' (Je. 1 :5, 9). In such ways God accommodated His inspiring work to the mind, outlook, concerns and style of each writer individually.

The divine dimension to Scripture in no way precludes normal methods of writing. Brunner contended that 'human research does exclude . . . divine inspiration', but Scripture does not bear him out. Luke wrote as the result of careful historical investigation into the events : 'it seemed good to me also, having followed all things closely for some time past, to write an orderly account . . .' (Lk. 1 :3). In places there is open acknowledgment of borrowing from non-canonical books. Equally there is evidence that a biblical book might 'pass through various editions and recensions over a period of centuries before reaching its final form' (cf. Pr. 10 :1; 24:23; 25 :1), as J. I. Packer has pointed out.

Thus the actual production of any part of Scripture is always to be viewed as the final stage or act in a series of processes – providential, gracious, supernatural and historical. This, taken as a whole, culminates in a recorded revelation in which words act as component parts of units of meaning. These units convey, through their human authors and features, the authentic and pure Word of God. The end result of all God's activity in this sphere of revelation and inspiration is the same as in every other area of His working : His end is perfectly achieved, for He is the One who works all things according to the counsel of His own will (Eph. 1 : 11).

When rightly understood, the phrase 'verbal inspiration' is not only appropriate to the nature of the Bible, but vital to its full import. It does not mean that you can pick out a word (or necessarily even a verse) from the middle of Proverbs and hold it up on its own for exhibit as an inspired word. That is to think atomistically, as though the words of the Bible were doled out to man one by one as individual pearls. Any word in Scripture is inspired only as part of the unit of meaning. To this unit it is absolutely essential, and at times a whole argument pivots on one word – indeed even on the distinction between singular and plural. See, for example, Galatians 3 :16, where Paul's teaching depends on 'offspring' being singular. Thus inspiration extends to the very words of Scripture – but to words as servants of phrases, sentences, arguments, books. Words are not ends in themselves and a veneration for words isolated from context and meaning is mere superstition.

But if God has spoken His saving truth to men in and through their language, then His words need our fullest attention. All words are symbols, the words of Scripture included; but the latter are so selected that to ignore or change the symbols is to bypass or distort the meaning. Hence the significance of the Holy Spirit superintending what David, Paul and the other writers expressed. It is part of God's saving grace that He has given us those units of meaning which together make up the unity of the Bible and accurately convey His voice to us.

CHAPTER SEVEN

FACING THE PROBLEMS

THE BIBLE is the Word of God : this is clearly the claim that it makes for itself. People may not always regard it in that way; and at times it may move and challenge us more than at others. But the variable is our will and understanding; the Bible is the constant. As God gave it, it is His Word. The Bible, not just some parts of it, is the Word of God; the Bible is, not merely may become, the Word of God; the Bible is God's Word, not the ideas of men.

If this is so, what of the objections to this view of inspiration? How may they be met? My aim now is to examine some of the arguments which are often raised against inspiration.

OBJECTIONS

(a) *'The internal evidence is lacking'*. Some assert that the Bible's own testimony does not yield or require such a view of itself. They can only uphold this assertion, however, if they ignore or deny the passages reviewed in the last chapter, and the many other passages like them. B. B. Warfield once illustrated the position in this way. You cannot, he said, avoid an avalanche merely by trying to dodge individual boulders; it is on an equally hopeless task to try to escape persistent internal testimony of the Bible to its own origin. More is required to undermine inspiration than even the 're-interpretation' of certain texts; the over-all perspective of the biblical writers has to be challenged.

(b) *'The New Testament writers misrepresented Christ'*. This is by no means clear on the face of the New Testament. This contention assumes that Christ was at variance, at least on this issue, with the apostles. This has to be assumed in order to be proved. If no such assumption is introduced, then no difficulty arises. We know no Christ except the Christ revealed through the writers. He bound His trustworthiness indissolubly to that of the apostles as His agents in conveying His truth and establishing His church (Jn. 16:12–15). If their teaching is incorrect on the basis and authority for faith, then where is it to be trusted?

(c) *'Christ and the apostles accommodated their teaching to Jewish belief'*. Christ did not merely *adapt* truth to the background and present capacity of His hearers, as any good teacher would; He actually *adopted* what (on this view) were the errors of the day as the matter to be taught.[1] Three points may be made. *First*, this assumes that Christ taught, but did not hold, a view of the Old Testament which was identical to the Jews' beliefs then. Even a superficial reading of the Gospels, however, dispels this view. Christ denounced the Jewish leaders for not holding to the true meaning of the Old Testament ('the commandment of God'), but rather to their own ideas ('the tradition of men', Mk. 7:1–13). Denunciation is a strange form of accommodation! *Second*, this affirms that Christ accommodated His teaching in order to try to win over the scribes and Pharisees; whereas He specifically says quite early in His ministry (Mk. 2:17) that He came not to call them ('the righteous') but sinners such as

[1] See B. B. Warfield, *The Inspiration and Authority of the Bible*, pp. 195 ff.

tax-collectors. *Third,* this infers that Christ's words are to be doubted whenever they coincide with Jewish belief – a somewhat puzzling position for a faith with its roots so firmly in the Old Testament.

(d) '*Verbal inspiration means the writers' personalities were eclipsed*'. God reduced them to mere scribes or typewriters and so inspiration is the equivalent of dictation. This appears plausible : if God was in control, the writers could not have been. We need first to note that, while Scripture speaks clearly on both its origin and nature, it is virtually silent as to the *mode* of its inspiration. What it seems to suggest is the *concursive* working of the Holy Spirit. This means that the human authors wrote freely and spontaneously, using to the full their minds, experiences and backgrounds; and yet at the same time they wrote 'words not taught by human wisdom but taught by the Spirit' (1 Cor. 2 : 13). The individuals were certainly not detached from God's control, but equally they were not men with blank minds or obliterated personalities. As we saw in the last chapter, God's long preparation of them even from before their birth would have been pointless if in the end their individuality was ruled out.

The initiation of spiritual life in an individual is a partial analogy to this. A person spiritually dead cannot in any way respond to God. But as the Holy Spirit gives new life, so the individual is enabled freely and spontaneously to repent, to turn to God and to believe in Christ. It is altogether the Spirit's work, but at the same time the response is personal to that individual and comes through the working of his mind and conscience and will.

(e) '*Perfect revelation cannot come through imperfect men*'. The argument is this: if God does *not* obliterate men's minds, how can they as fallible mortals convey God's infallible truth? One answer to this we have already seen : the fact of God preparing these men to be precisely His intended instruments for this work. But an even more basic issue is involved – the question of the nature and power of God. Are we to believe that God was limited by men? That He was inhibited, hindered and even frustrated in His revealing purpose by having to work through imperfect human material? If men can in fact tie God's hands in this way, then God can never communicate His mind accurately to men. At the very least, Scripture never gave birth to this caricature, this affront to the sovereign power of God. If men were sovereign, then perfect revelation could never come; it *has* come because God is reigning.

(f) *'Verbal inspiration does not allow for oral tradition'*. Space forbids any extended treatment of this, but the position may be summarized as follows. Clearly the church first had the original revelation in the form of the actual words and deeds of Christ. This was continued in the days immediately after Christ's ascension through the words of the apostles : an oral tradition. When finally this was cast by the apostles themselves into written form, the formation of this *graphē* spelt the end of oral tradition. As Cullmann indicated, the New Testament is not a second body of traditions alongside another ongoing stream of tradition; it is the embodiment of all true extant revelations and traditions. To stress oral tradition at the expense of the written, or to pit one against the other, is to deny the very reasons which led the apostles to create a Christian Scripture.

(g) *'Verbal inspiration leads to a religion of the letter, not of the Spirit'*. It makes faith bookish, intellectualistic and impersonal. After all, Paul said : 'The written code kills, but the Spirit gives life' (2 Cor. 3 :6). This passage is often used as an argument in this matter, so we must note what Paul was referring to here. It was not to the

Old Testament as such, but specifically to the ten commandments. These were 'a dispensation of death' when regarded as a setting out of God's standards. Their function was to kill stone-dead men's hopes of self-righteousness, so that they might come to receive life through the Spirit. The really significant fact for this objection is this: in both 'dispensations' (that of death and that of the Spirit) there is the written word. The difference is not that one is written down and the other is not; the difference is that the former is *only* written whereas the latter is *also* written into the human heart by the Spirit. True faith rests on an objectively true written revelation; and also on the Spirit removing the veil from our minds to enable us to perceive and respond to what is 'there' (*cf.* 2 Cor. 3 : 14–16). Word and Spirit go together to promote spiritual life, as William Cowper wrote :

> The Spirit breathes upon the Word,
> And brings the truth to sight;
> Precepts and promises afford
> A sanctifying light.

(h) '*Verbal inspiration produces bibliolatry, a paper pope*'. Some contend that after the Reformation the absolute authority of the church through the papacy was replaced by the bare authority of the book and go on to add that both equally are to be deplored. No-one would deny that veneration of a book as mere paper and ink is to be decried, for that would separate Scripture from God. Just as we may not do that, neither may we separate God's voice from Scripture. If the one is bibliolatry, the other is mysticism. Both are erroneous, for it is God who is to be worshipped – the God who speaks in Scripture. If it has pleased God to breathe out the Bible and make it in every part His revelation, then it is no crime so to view it. That is the test.

(i) *'There is doubt about the formation of the canon'.*
The idea of a canon (meaning measuring rod, rule or
standard) is essential if we are to be able to know certainly
what God has said. Yet the very idea raises difficulties.
The statement 'all scripture is inspired by God' does not
itself tell us what books are or are not part of Scripture.
It is no secret that certain books were at times disputed,
notably Esther and the Song of Solomon in the Old
Testament, and Jude, 2 and 3 John and Philemon in the
New. How then can we be sure about the present canon?
In this brief survey three points may be noted.

First, *the very idea of a canon is necessarily implied in
the idea of inspiration.* That is, if God breathed out any
books at all, they must be the rule or standard for faith.
In this sense any inspired book was canonical from the
time it was produced, whether or not it was so recognized
at once. This is the basic fact concerning canonicity. The
church neither could nor did confer status on a book, since
God had already made it authoritative by producing it.
The church had and has no authority over the Bible;
rather, the exact reverse. The church can no more make a
book authoritative than it can cause men to manufacture
God's words. It was God who created the canon.

Second, *the limits of the Old Testament canon.* It has
often been thought that the Council of Jamnia (*c.* AD 100)
fixed these. But the evidence does no more than show that
informal discussions on this subject were held at that
centre of Jewish scholarship. No official or binding decrees emerged. In fact the limits of the Old Testament
canon are decisively fixed for us by our Lord's own view.
He regarded the whole Old Testament as we know it as
the Word of God (*cf.* Jn. 10 :31–36; Lk. 24 :44). Interest-
ingly He did not differ from the Pharisees about the authority of the Old Testament; He disagreed with the
addition of their traditions to it.

Even within the Old Testament, however, there are references showing that its parts were regarded as divinely authoritative. The Book of the Law was to be positioned beside the very ark of the covenant. The words of the prophets called for an obedience proper only to God's voice. Ezra 7 :6 records that Ezra was 'a scribe skilled in the law of Moses which the Lord the God of Israel had given'. Patently the law of Moses was already regarded as canonical, having originated with God. Similarly in Nehemiah 10 :29 we read that the people entered into 'a curse and an oath to walk in God's law which was given by Moses the servant of God, and to observe and do all the commandments of the Lord . . .' Ezra and Nehemiah bestowed no new status on these books; they merely recognized them as 'God's law'.

Third, *the limits of the New Testament canon*. The church was never without a canon, for the obvious reason that it inherited and accepted the Old Testament. The question is not how the New Testament writings became canonical or binding, for that question is answered by their inspiration. The canon was completed when the last authoritative book was given to any church by the apostles.[2] The question is : how did they come to be recognized as equally canonical with those of the Old Testament?

Clearly the churches did not all acquire copies of all the books at the same time. Incomplete canons circulated in some areas for a period, for the unavoidable reason that the process of manuscript copying was so slow and painstaking. Partly for this reason, certain books were questioned within limited areas (*e.g.* Hebrews in the Western church and Revelation in the Eastern). The whole canon was not recognized everywhere until into the fourth cen-

[2] *Cf.* B. B. Warfield, *op. cit.*, p. 415.

tury; for example, in AD 367 Athanasius defined the limits of the New Testament exactly as we know them.

However, the evidence of early Christian fragments is 'enough to show that the collection in general use (at the opening of the second century) contained all the books which we at present receive, with the possible exceptions of Jude, 2 and 3 John and Philemon. And it is more natural to suppose that failure of very early evidence for these brief booklets is due to their insignificant size rather than to their non-acceptance.'[3] Polycarp in AD 115, then Clement and later others, quote from Old and New Testaments in terms of 'as it is said in these scriptures'.[4]

By what standards then were works received as canonical? Apostolic authorship certainly came into it. Hesitation about this in respect of Hebrews, James and Jude caused delay in their acceptance in some churches. However, 'the principle of canonicity was not apostolic authorship but *imposition by the apostles as "law"* . . . The authority of the apostles, as by divine appointment founders of the church, was embodied in whatever they imposed on the church as law, not merely in those they themselves had written.'[5] The books of the New Testament did not gradually rise to equal status with those of the Old; they had it intrinsically from the start.

We may not know all the details about the acceptance of the canon; what we do know leaves no doubt that the whole canon is to be received as the inspired word of God.

(j) *'The inspiration of the Bible is so uneven'*. Every professing Christian would agree that Psalm 23 is inspired and inspiring. The case seems rather different, for ex-

[3] B. B. Warfield, *op. cit.*, p. 414.
[4] *Cf.* B. B. Warfield, *op. cit.*, p. 412; article on 'The Canon of the New Testament' in *The New Bible Dictionary*; and *Revelation and the Bible* (ed. C. F. H. Henry), pp. 197–201.
[5] B. B. Warfield, *op. cit.*, pp. 415–6.

ample, in Ezra 2 when sixty-one verses are taken up with a list of those who returned from exile. In the light of such lists and genealogies, it is hard to hold that all Scripture is equally inspired.

We need to remember that each part of the Bible has its own particular purpose within the whole. Features may be proper to the nature and purpose of a historical section which would be utterly incongruous in the Psalms. This does not deny the inspiration of either; it simply recognizes their distinctive literary form and intent. Just imagine the situation if all the parts of questionable inspiration or value were excised from Scripture. History stripped of genealogies and other lists would appear, by comparison with other literature from their Ancient Near Eastern background, to be very strange. Doubt would be cast on the genuineness of the books. Of course, some might still contend that nothing of devotional value would be lost. We cannot be quite so sure. When he was starting to open up Matthew to his congregation, one preacher could not do other than start with the first seventeen verses. These give the genealogy of Christ and, improbable as it may seem, one person was converted through that sermon. 'I suddenly came to see from this that Christ was a real person.'

Inspiration means that all Scripture is profitable. It does not teach that it is all profitable in the same way or for the same detailed purposes.

A DEFINITION

To close our treatment of inspiration, we offer a possible definition with some explanatory comments : *Inspiration means that God the Holy Spirit worked in a unique supernatural way so that the written words of the Scripture writers were also the words of God.*

God the Holy Spirit : it is He who produced Scripture. While this may tell us little about the actual mode of its formation, it does tell us about its origin and nature (a book breathed out by God). The Bible is thus God's Word. This does not lead us to venerate the book rather than the Author, but simply to reverence and obey the One whose voice is Scripture. Inspiration essentially means that what Scripture says, God says.

Unique : inspiration is a distinctive work of the Spirit and is not to be confused with His 'ordinary', everyday work. This latter consists, for example, in giving new life to non-Christians, instructing and strengthening Christians and building up Christ's body. Inspiration, though from the same Spirit, relates exclusively to the producing of Scripture and is thus *extra-ordinary* and unique.

Supernatural : that is, the inspiration of the writers is not on the same level or of the same kind as poetic or artistic inspiration. It is one thing to have an inspired piece of music or to run an inspired race in athletics; these are heightened forms of ordinary human consciousness or activity. The Bible, however, is supernatural in that it is breathed out and sent down by God, not thought up by men.

Written : inspiration refers to writing, recording. It is thus distinguishable from revelation; revelation is the imparting or disclosing of truth, inspiration is the recording, preserving and conveying of it. B. B. Warfield wrote: 'Revelation is but half revelation unless it be infallibly *communicated*; it is but half communicated unless it be infallibly *recorded*. The heathen in their blindness are our witnesses of what becomes of an unrecorded revelation. Let us bless God, then, for His inspired word !'[6]

Writers : The entire Bible (and not just parts of it) has

[6] *Op. cit.*, p. 442.

a human aspect. It came into being through human literary processes. It was written by men. To be sure, they were men whom God chose, prepared and used; but they did not cease to be conscious, thoughtful, responsible individuals. They wrote freely and spontaneously so that what was God's word was also fully their word.

Words: Inspiration thus effects words which are at once divine and human. All were given through men, all are in human language, yet all are bearers of divine truth. They convey His voice as they form units of meaning, individual phrases and sentences being built together into the particular book; all the books are equally integrated into the entire book, God's one sufficient body of saving truth for men.

DEVOTION

This means something tremendous for the Christian's devotion. God has not given us a book of abstract theological propositions or bare philosophical concepts. Neither has He allowed us to have a book of unaided human speculation about the eternal and the infinite. The first would have been true, but not earthed in our life; the second would have been earthed, but not true. As it is, God has favoured us with a book which is both true (because breathed out) and earthed (because written by men in and out of human life and experience). We may thus find eternal truth directly related to temporal situations. We read of the unchangeable God in His dealings with changeable men and women. We learn of the Holy One in His relation to people who have similar failings and desires to our own. This is God's infinite condescension to us. The divine-human nature of the Bible is much more than an academic theological assertion or a stage in an argument about the Bible. It is not just a good excuse to keep the pot of theological debate boiling. It is the great fact which brings God to us and us to God in a living, growing and glorious personal relationship with Him.

CHAPTER EIGHT

INFALLIBLE TRUTH?

SO FAR we have discussed three basic facts:

Fact one: God could not be discovered by man's unaided reason.

Fact two: God has revealed Himself both in action in human history and in word in human language.

Fact three: God has worked in a unique, supernatural way so that the written words of Scripture are also His words.

The question now is: what do these facts mean about the Bible? In particular, what are the implications of the Bible being 'God-breathed'?

If we reply that these facts mean that the Bible is God's infallible truth, some Christians are immediately puzzled or embarrassed. The meaning of such a term seems elusive, its basis looks shaky . . . and does it really fit the facts about the Bible? To some it seems rather a side issue anyway, since many people profess to believe in revelation and inspiration and yet reject this.

What then is the position? Any piece of writing, and particularly perhaps an autobiography or an educational book, shares and demonstrates its author's character. If he is misguided, his book will reflect the fact; if he is not, the book will have a different character. This is a plain matter of fact and observation. And, because the Bible is literature, it has the same characteristics.

To put it in its most basic terms, the question of whether

or not the Bible is God's infallible truth turns on two issues : (a) the Bible's origin, *i.e.* whether in fact the Bible came from God and was breathed out by Him; and (b) God's nature, *i.e.* whether God is infallible.

This is to say that if God Himself breathed out the Bible, so that it is His voice; and if He is the God who cannot lie, then His book is as true and trustworthy (that is to say, as infallible) as He is. By this we mean negatively that the Bible is not misleading and positively that its meaning is wholly reliable. To accept the Bible as inspired by God leads naturally and necessarily to accepting it as sharing God's infallible character.

Much more remains to be said on this matter, but it is important to clarify one point at the outset. This view adds nothing new or incongruous to the fact of inspiration. It merely makes explicit what *theopneustos* inescapably implies. It is not like a P.S. added to a letter on a completely different subject; it is part of the letter itself. The two notions ('inspired' and 'infallible') stand or fall together. To reject the one is to undermine the other. To attempt to retain a true view of inspiration while refusing the concept of 'the infallible truth'[1] of Holy Scripture is bound to result in a radically lower view of inspiration than the Bible itself propounds. This is not therefore an isolated notion tacked on to the doctrine of Scripture by extremists; it is firmly grounded in the facts of revelation and inspiration. In practice each person's concept of inspiration settles one way or the other their view of this issue.

Now we recognize that the term 'infallible' itself seems to cloud the issue at times. To the Protestant it smacks of the papacy and so carries an unwelcome association of ideas. But we should not and do not hesitate to speak of

[1] *The Confession of Faith* of 1647 (the 'Westminster Confession'), I.v.

God as infallible. This idea is unmistakably present wherever God's nature is revealed to us in Scripture. It is there when we read that 'God cannot lie', that His 'word endures for ever'. It confronts us in Christ's words : 'I am the way, the *truth* and the life'. It is exclusively in association with God's character that the term is to be grasped and used. It cannot be overstressed in any discussion of this matter that its meaning derives from God's truthfulness and integrity.

Our purpose now therefore is not to argue for the Bible as God's infallible word. The arguments for this are those for inspiration. Rather here our purpose is to draw out the implications of the Bible being breathed out by God and so to think through the meaning of 'infallible' as it may be applied to the Bible.

THE PURPOSE OF THE BIBLE

Paul wrote that Scripture is 'able to instruct you for salvation . . . and profitable for teaching, for reproof, for correction, and for training in righteousness, that the man of God may be complete, equipped for every good work' (2 Tim. 3 : 15–17). Jesus said that the Scriptures 'bear witness to me' and implied that the Jews were right to think that 'in them you have eternal life' (Jn. 5 : 39). After His resurrection He spoke to the two on the road to Emmaus : 'And beginning with Moses and all the prophets, he interpreted to them in all the scriptures the things concerning himself' (Lk. 24 : 27).

These and other references tell us that God has selected the contents of the Bible for us. *Negatively* this means two things : on the one hand God has not given us an exhaustive self-disclosure; on the other hand He has not made Scripture a general knowledge encyclopaedia, a look-within-on-everything. The Bible does not tell us the times of high tides at Scarborough, the maximum safe size of oil tankers or the exact nature of the moon's surface. *Positively* this means that in the Bible God has given to men a sufficient knowledge of Himself and His will so that they may enter a right relationship with Him and know how to live, think and act in this world. All that God deemed necessary to that purpose is in the Bible; all that He deemed unnecessary is excluded. The whole Bible is thus an expression of the principle spoken of in Deuteronomy 29:29 : 'The secret things belong to the Lord our God; but the things that are revealed belong to us and to our children for ever, that we may do all the words of this law.' The primary truth is that the Bible is infallible in terms of what it is and what it is for.

While this is the essential purpose of Scripture, how-ever, we must not prejudge what Scripture does and does not speak of. Some have, mistakenly, jumped to the con-clusion that only the spiritual or religious assertions of the book are true and that its statements about fact and his-tory are not necessarily so. Others have come to a pietistic position : the Bible speaks to them for the purposes of their individual devotional life, but only for that. Since it does not speak in as many words about many modern prob-lems, they feel it can be ignored in all but our religious life.

If we want to discern the purpose of the Bible and therefore the extent of its infallibility, we must be very careful to let Scripture itself explain these things to us and define their limits. It would not be difficult to list any number of topics on which there is no verse in the Bible and which you would not find in a concordance : labour relations in industry, the philosophy of science, denomina-tional loyalty, euthanasia or when to change your job. It does not follow, as we hope to show later, that the Bible has nothing of relevance to say to such issues. This leads us to the next aspect.

THE WRITERS' INTENTION

Our task is to note in each passage what each writer intended to convey; or, to be more exact, what the Holy Spirit speaking through the writer intended to convey. That, and that only, is His infallible truth. This of course has reference to that method of finding 'guidance' which, opening the Bible quite at random, lifts a verse right out of context and finds God's direction in it. A missionary once had to get from A to B, but did not know whether to go by air or sea; opening the Bible, it fell open at Isaiah 40 and verse 31 seemed to stand out : 'they shall mount up with wings like eagles'. So the answer was clear : fly ! Now it may well have been right for that person to fly on that occasion, but it is more than doubtful whether that was the intention behind Isaiah 40 : 31.

We must note the writers' intentions therefore; but in practice we are sometimes strangely slow to do so. For example, we sometimes have a very wooden, unthinking approach to the reporting of speeches or events in Scripture. True reports may come in different ways : one may be *verbatim*, another condensed to give the salient points, a third selective (reporting one particular person or theme, or reporting for a distinctive group). Imagine a speech by a church leader on relations between the denominations. One Anglican newspaper might report it from quite a different perspective within Anglicanism from another. An interdenominational paper would narrate it for the general Christian public. A Methodist or Baptist paper might highlight references to their denominations. Now all these might be found to misrepresent the speech; but there is nothing in principle to prevent five differing reports all being equally true if understood in relation to the reporter's purpose. None would be a word-for-word account, for in certain circumstances (*e.g.* readers who knew little of the background) even that might be confusing and misleading. But the readers of each paper would expect their reporter to write truly of what concerned them; and understanding his intention as not to give a *verbatim* account, but rather a selective one, they would not be misled.

Take two examples. If a Scripture writer's professed or discernible intention is to offer a selective account, it is no argument against the Bible being God's infallible truth to point out that he does not include every word or incident. This is illustrated in the three accounts of the healing of the epileptic following the transfiguration. May not the differences be sufficiently accounted for by observing the particular stress of each writer? Matthew stresses the little faith of the disciples (17 : 19,20); Mark that it requires prayer (9 : 28,29); and Luke that Christ's action displayed the majesty of God (9 : 43).

Another example is Paul's use of the phrase 'in heaven and on earth and under the earth' (Phil. 2 : 10). Some believe that Paul held to a three-decker universe and conclude, obviously enough on that assumption, that he was mistaken. But what is the passage about? Paul is exhorting Christians to be 'of the same mind, having the same love, being in full accord and of one mind'. He is urging them : 'in humility count others better than yourselves.' Then he presents the example of Christ who humbled Himself, and is led on to speak of the day when *everyone* will acknowledge that Christ is Lord. Now is he really teaching a three-decker universe as an article of Christian belief? Or is he using a current phrase to convey how utterly *comprehensive* will be the ultimate acknowledgment of Christ? He is not advocating an obsolete cosmology; he is using a popular and passing phrase to convey an abiding truth. He was writing to be understood by his readers then. This implies a distinction between the meaning a writer intends to convey and the form of expression in which he transmits it.

This procedure, adopted in varying degrees throughout Scripture, is to be sharply distinguished from that of 'demythologization'. We may recognize the distinction between meaning and form of expression, but this does not deny or call in question the whole outlook on life of the biblical writers. For some, however, this distinction is not radical enough. According to Rudolf Bultmann and others, we must at the start rule out as mythical the total world-view of the writers, and with it all that is supernatural or miraculous. All that comes in those categories must be jettisoned in order to expose for modern scientific man a gospel which is credible. Thus the pre-existence of Christ, the virgin birth, substitutionary death and bodily resurrection must go. We must have a 'truth which is quite independent of its mythological setting'.[2]

Such presuppositions have clearly influenced the approach to the Bible and were not learnt from it. By contrast, we must seek rather to discern and submit to the intention of each part of the Bible. It may not always be easy to distinguish an ephemeral phrase from the abiding truth, but three factors need to be remembered. First, straightforward study of a passage often makes the answer clear, as when examining Philippians 2 : 10 in the light of the whole chapter. Second, if there are problems in this sphere, they must be seen in proportion, for they relate mainly to the finer points of exegesis. Third, this is not a question that directly impinges on whether the Bible is God's infallible truth; it is essentially a question of how to understand what each part of Scripture is asserting.

[2] R. Bultmann, *Kerygma and Myth*, p. 3.

THE USE OF LANGUAGE

Allied to this is the writers' use of words and phrases. They wrote for the populace and their language was popular. They wrote to be understood and frequently used idioms. We saw in chapter 5 how the Bible's language is marked by the use of analogy, and often they describe things as they appear rather than as they actually are. Because of this it is rightly said that the Bible's language is pre- or non-scientific. Yet it is doubtful whether this comment is particularly relevant. Are we to suppose that, had the Bible been written this year, it would have analysed our latest knowledge of the solar system when it simply wanted to indicate that 'the sun rose'? Even in this scientific age we are obscurantist enough to talk of the sun 'rising', of Australia as being 'down under' and of someone having 'his heart in his mouth'. Thus it is no surprise that the Bible speaks, as we have seen, of 'the finger of God', 'the pillars of the earth' or things 'in heaven and on earth and under the earth'.

Such phrases are misleading if taken in a superficial, literalistic sense. But, and this is the point, they convey meaning reliably when taken as they were intended. We thus have to distinguish between the subjects on which the Bible speaks and the forms of speech in which it describes them. Human traits and idioms are perfectly consistent with the infallible truth of the Bible. 'Inspiration is a means to an end and not an end in itself; if the truth is accurately conveyed to the ear that listens to it, its full end is obtained.'[3]

[3] B. B. Warfield, *The Inspiration and Authority of the Bible*, p. 438.

INFALLIBLE TRUTH AND INTERPRETATION

The infallible message of the Bible must be rightly discerned, the inspired sense rightly interpreted. The Bible's message cannot automatically be identified with the surface sense of an isolated passage. Obviously, any *mis*-understanding of the Bible will *mis*lead. When the sects (and others!) lift phrases or verses out of their context, they have no ground for claiming that their views are trustworthy. Only when any passage is rightly grasped in relation to its context and purpose do we arrive at the unerring truth that part enshrines. We shall look later at principles of interpretation, but here we must recognize the distinction between the trustworthiness of the Bible as such, and the trustworthiness (or otherwise) of any particular interpretation of it. To submit to the rule of Scripture does not bind anyone to accept all the interpretations of anyone else who also seeks to sit under its authority. This does not mean that the Bible's meaning is obscure. It does not mean that objective principles of understanding the Bible are lacking. It does signal the fact that the Bible has often been misinterpreted and that we must seek the Spirit's help to comply with Paul's command : 'Do your best to present yourself to God as one approved, a workman who has no need to be ashamed, rightly handling (lit. cutting straight or right) the word of truth' (2 Tim. 2 : 15).

CHAPTER NINE

MATTERS OF FACT

IN THE LIGHT of what we have seen, how are we to regard the factual references in the Bible? Did the events recorded as history really happen? What of the variations between different accounts of the same event or speech? Are the references to numbers and dates accurate?

This is the question we must face : is the Bible God's infallible truth only in its general teaching, or does it also possess inerrancy in detailed, lesser matters?

We believe the evidence shows that it does, and it is worth noting that this has been the general consensus in the church's teaching from the beginning. This view is no novelty. It was not produced as a reaction to liberal views in this or the last century. Similarly, almost all the alleged objections to it have an archaic ring to them; most of them have been well known for centuries. This has in fact been the church's teaching because it was already taught in New Testament times. It is helpful to see how the New Testament writers regarded Old Testament history.

The events recorded were ordered by God both for the benefit of His people then and for our instruction now. 'These things (in this instance the historical events under Moses) are warnings for us . . . Now these things happened to them as a warning, but they were written down for our instruction . . .' (1 Cor. 10 :6, 11). These events actually took place, and history moved forward as it did under God's hand. It did so to bear a warning to them and a message to us. Jesus makes similar references to Old Testament history, *e.g.* the events in the life of Jonah and Solomon (Mt. 12:38–40) and the fate of Sodom and Gomorrah (Mt. 11:20–24). These events happened and, because of their historicity, still have definite lessons to teach. They are more than illustrations; they are historical parallels to convey how God acted and still acts.

God brought about the events and, as we saw earlier, moved His appointed men to record them. Both the events and the record are reliable. This is precisely what we should expect, since God's saving acts and His saving revelation are so inextricably interwoven. To imagine that the message is reliable but that the events (through which the Scripture writers assert that it was delivered) did not take place is quite as difficult as to believe in the authenticity of both. Think of it like this: if men whom God moved could prophesy truly for many hundreds of years ahead, could they not at least as readily record accurately what had already happened?

This is not to deny the problems, and we must squarely face the charge that there are proven errors in the Bible. I want therefore to take three main areas where difficulties arise concerning the belief that the Bible is infallible and inerrant. Isolated examples will not convince those who are already disposed to believe that errors exist. They may, however, be of use to those who seek to know whether and how such problem passages fit in with what the Bible teaches about itself. The examples can only be surveyed briefly here, with some indications of how such disputed areas may be approached. The three areas are those of the Old Testament, the use of the Old in the New, and the New itself.

THE OLD TESTAMENT

First *the Old Testament's use of numbers*. At least two factors must be considered :

(a) The first concerns the writer's meaning again. Saul, David and Solomon are recorded as having each reigned for forty years; the book of Judges repeats that the land had rest for forty years (Jdg. 3 :11; 5 :31; 8 :28). Did the writers intend us to take each period as exactly forty years down to the last hour, minute and second? Are we not rather to understand this as an idiomatic expression, 'forty' standing for a generation in round figures, or for quite a considerable period?

(b) The second factor relates to the transmission of the text. When numbers, as in the Old Testament, are written as words, there is the possibility of error in transcription. Hebrew was written with consonants only; the vowels, the 'points', were omitted. Thus the word for a thousand (*elep̄*), if otherwise vocalized, means 'captain' (*allup̄*). To give an example, this could make the difference in 1 Chronicles 12 between reading it as the '50,000 of Zebulun, or as the '50 captains of Zebulun'.

These limited examples illustrate how particular problems may be tackled : by attention to questions of style, language and transmission. Many such problems have been resolved when new discoveries shed light on textual or historical factors previously unknown. While it is obvious that we do not yet have solutions to all the detailed questions, it is also obvious that many problems have been resolved over the years. It is not the puzzling details that should determine our total attitude. In any case, these are questions of how to arrive at the correct reading or how to understand the text. As we saw in the last chapter, there is a distinction between infallible truth and interpretation. Problems of understanding (and relatively they are very minor indeed) encountered *en route* do not call in question the existence of the destination.

Second under the heading of Old Testament problems are *the occasions when the biblical records seem to conflict*. Leon Morris has written : 'Where one biblical writer is set against another (or against himself) the position is difficult. Perhaps we might take as a typical example of this type of objection that which points out that in one place we read, "the anger of Jehovah was kindled against Israel, and he moved David against them, saying, Go, number Israel and Judah" (2 Sam. 24 : 1), while in another, which tells of the same incident, "Satan stood up against Israel, and moved David to number Israel" (1 Chron. 21 : 1). The Chronicler did not like the theology he found in his source, we are told, and therefore he corrected it.

'But it is possible to see the two passages in another light. From one point of view it was Satan who moved David to this act. There was something wrong in it (even if we do not discern exactly what the evil was), and thus it came from the evil one. But from another point of view the hand of God must be seen in it. It is the uniform picture in Scripture that Satan has no absolute power. He can operate only within the limits that God prescribes. But if God permits his activities there is a sense in which He is responsible. He may even be termed the author of these activities.'[1]

---

[1] 'Biblical Authority and the Concept of Inerrancy', *The Churchman*, 81.1 (Spring 1967), p. 27. For suggestions on how to approach other Old Testament passages seemingly difficult to reconcile, *cf.* E. J. Young, *Thy Word is Truth*, pp. 119–126. There he tackles the relationship between Gn. 1 and 2, Is. 2 : 1–4 and Mi. 4 : 1–3, and the problem of whether or not the high places were removed (1 Ki. 15 : 14 and 2 Ch. 14 : 5).

THE OLD TESTAMENT IN THE NEW

How does the New Testament use the Old? If it quoted exactly and literally, there would be little to discuss. As it is, the quotations seem somewhat loose and inexact. Two general remarks are relevant before we look at particular examples.

(a) We must remember that there are various ways in which quotations may be given, just as there are various ways of reporting an incident. It is not necessary for accuracy in English that the exact words should be enclosed within quotation marks. That, of course, is the most obvious method to use, yet it can be just as accurate to summarize what was said or even to select certain phrases for emphasis. When I have been reading a good book and want to tell someone else about it, I can say: 'This is what he says on page 84, paragraph 3 . . .' and then proceed to read that section. Equally I could say: 'The writer says that . . .' and go on to summarize his meaning. Again, if the other person knows something about the book, he might ask: 'Does the hero come out on top?' My reply would then effectively be quotation, even though it were merely Yes or No.

(b) We must always keep in mind the writer's intention. The Spirit's work in inspiration secures only that the writer does what he, guided by the Spirit, sets out to do. If an author does not claim to quote the Old Testament *verbatim*, it is no objection to the truth of inspiration that he does not give the *ipsissima verba*. If it is adequate for his purposes to give the general sense, *e.g.* of Christ's words, or a valid aspect of that sense, this is not inconsistent with inspiration. Only if he professed to give the actual words and did not would an objection arise.

This must preface consideration of how to regard inexact quotation within Scripture. As E. J. Young points out, the first citation of the Old in the New poses a problem. Matthew 1 :23 does not give *verbatim* the words of Isaiah 7 :14. Matthew seems to have followed the Septuagint (the Greek version of the Old Testament) rather than the Hebrew; and to have used the Greek for virgin (*parthenos*) when there is no word in Hebrew which *exclusively* connotes virgin. We sometimes find, as in this case, that New Testament writers give the sense (or even one aspect of the sense) of the original, rather than a rigid translation. This does not mean that they have misled us concerning the original.

Another difficulty in Matthew may be cited. In 27 :9–10 the prophecy of Zechariah 11 :13 introduced by the words, 'Then was fulfilled what had been spoken by the prophet Jeremiah, saying . . .' The two problems are the inexact quotation and the attribution to Jeremiah. One answer has been proposed on these lines : Matthew was obviously reflecting on the fate of Judas. The buying of the *potter's* field could well have turned his mind back to the symbolism of Jeremiah 18 and 19, the great passage on the potter and the clay. This ends with a reference to God breaking His people and the city Jerusalem, as one breaks a potter's vessel (19 :10–13). Zechariah 11 :13 would also come to his mind because of the reference to the thirty pieces of silver. So Matthew sums it all up in his free quotation which he gives under the name of the greater of the two prophets. After all, the better a person knows his sources, the more freely can he use them without misrepresentation. Another suggestion is that the Evangelist was using a Testimony book which began with quotations from Jeremiah and ended with some from Zechariah.

In Ephesians 4 :8 Paul is referring to Christ's triumph and ascension. He alludes to Psalm 68 :18 and this raises a difficulty. In the Psalm the writer is speaking of God's victory on the people's behalf, and speaks of God in consequence 'receiving gifts among men'. Paul quotes this, however, as 'he gave gifts to men'. Now it is undeniable that giving is the opposite of receiving. But before we close the issue there, another solution may be considered. It is this : did not Christ first receive in order that He might give? This would accord with what we read elsewhere, *e.g.* 'God has highly exalted him and *bestowed* on him' the supreme name (Phil. 2 :9); and He was '*crowned* with glory and honour' (Heb. 2 :9). Certainly Paul's quotation is not word-for-word; but the sense is not abused.

This does not mean that the New Testament writers sat loose to the inspiration and inerrancy of the Old. They quoted as they did under the moving of the same Holy Spirit to convey what He purposed. It was He who prompted them to write as they did. The inference is unwarranted that the wording of the Old Testament is a matter of indifference.

In this matter of quotations we must remember that it is not merely a problem between Old and New Testaments. Within a single chapter our Lord, having made a statement, then gives an altered version as a quotation of the first statement. John 6 :44 reads : 'No one can come to me unless the Father who sent me draws him.' John 6 :65 reads : 'This is why I told you that no one can come to me unless it is granted him by the Father.' It might be thought pure pedantry to raise two such verses. Obviously the sense is the same; people are entirely dependent on the Father to come to know Christ. Yet our point is this : such procedure is no different in principle from that which we have seen employed by New Testament writers quoting the Old. The one should cause no greater difficulty than the other.

THE NEW TESTAMENT

We need now to face some of the alleged contradictions in the Gospels. We offer three of these as not untypical of the rest.

First, the case of *the ruler who asked Christ a question* (Mt. 19:16ff.; Mk. 10:17ff.; Lk. 18:18ff.). Matthew reads: 'Why do you ask me about what is good?' Luke records: 'Why do you call me good?' As they stand, these are two different questions; this does not necessarily mean that one must be wrong. If anyone had to prove here that either intended to give a *verbatim* account, he would be hard pressed to do so. And if we are not to take the reports as such, then it is possible to conceive how both reported questions arose directly out of Christ's words. Christ was good; eternal life was also good; therefore goodness could easily be attributed to both. Thus each account supplements the other. Both are true accounts though neither is *verbatim*. Why must we have slavish imitation in order to have inerrancy?

Second, *the mission of the twelve* (Mt. 10:5–10; Mk. 6:7–9; Lk. 9:1–3). The commands concerning staff and sandals pose two problems. Take the sandals first: these are commanded in Mark, forbidden in Matthew. The general import of Christ's commission was that the twelve were not to take unnecessary clothing. A reconciliation could be along the lines that they were to take the sandals they had on, but not a spare pair (*cf.* 'nor two tunics', Mt. 10:10). That this is not special pleading is shown by the verbs used. The verb in Matthew (*ktaomai*) means 'to provide for oneself, to acquire', whereas that in Mark (*airō*) means simply 'to take'.

What of the staff? It was permitted in Mark, prohibited in Matthew and Luke. Again, a harmonization may be on similar lines: that the twelve were to take their existing staffs, but not purchase new ones for the journey. M. Eaton has suggested another possibility. The reason for not taking an (extra) staff in Matthew is : 'for the labourer deserves his food (*trophē*)'. In fact *trophē* may bear a sense (of 'living', 'support') wider than merely food. The meaning therefore is that the apostles would expect to have their meals provided for them. Thus the command in Matthew is not that the apostles should not take a staff, but that the staff they take should not be one of their own provision. As this suggestion arises independently of harmonizing requirements, it has much to commend it.

Third, *the suicide of Judas* (Mt. 27 :3–10; Acts 1 : 19, 20). This is too involved to discuss fully here. However, it is worth summarizing the results of the meticulous study of this made by J. S. Baxter.[2] He found grounds for a solution of the three main problems as follows. (a) The problem of the purchase of the field : the chief priests made their purchase after the crucifixion, Judas his sometime before. (b) The problem of the suicide : Judas did hang himself and, after some time, his body fell of its own weight and burst open. (c) The problem of the fulfilment : this we have already touched on above.

We have offered some suggested harmonizations of passages. The harmonizations are possible, even probable. Other harmonizations may come to light, and we must allow that a harmony may exist even when we cannot see it yet.

This means that we are not bound, in order to retain a full persuasion of the Bible's inerrancy, to be able to demonstrate the harmony in every case. 'If we cannot har-

---

[2] *Studies in Problem Texts*, pp. 133–147. The chapter is well worth consulting on the whole approach to apparently irreconcilable passages.

monize without straining, let us leave unharmonized.'[3] Special pleading has no place. However, if harmonizations are demonstrably fitting on exegetical and other grounds in many cases, there is even less reason to deny harmony where we may not yet have perceived it.

Thus, although we have proposed some approaches to apparent discrepancies, we must in the nature of the case be prepared for unresolved problems. In almost every case these concern details and incidentals only.

The real issues, however, are whether any problems are to be regarded as incapable of solution, and whether there are any proven errors. Only if a problem is finally insoluble and is actually established as an error does any objection arise against the inerrancy of the Bible. Think for a moment about what needs to be demonstrated concerning a 'difficulty' in order to transfer it into the category of a valid argument against this doctrine. Certainly much more is required than the mere *appearance* of a contradiction. First, we must be certain that we have correctly understood the passage, the sense in which it uses words or numbers. Second, that we possess all available knowledge in this matter. Third, that no further light can possibly be thrown on it by advancing knowledge, textual research, archaeology, *etc*.

Put at its simplest, our point is (and it has been made by many before) that difficulties do not constitute objections. Unsolved problems are not of necessity errors. This is not to minimize the area of difficulty; it is to see it in perspective. Difficulties are to be grappled with and problems are to drive us to seek clearer light; but until such time as we have total and final light on any issue we are in no position to affirm, 'Here is a proven error, an unquestionable objection to an infallible Bible.' It is com-

[3] B. B. Warfield, *The Inspiration and Authority of the Bible*, p. 219.

mon knowledge that countless 'objections' have been fully resolved since this century began. Are we now to say that the residual problems cannot now or ever be solved? Such is hardly a scientific attitude, let alone a Christian one.

It sometimes seems to be taken as axiomatic that we cannot accept the Bible until all our queries about it have been cleared away. We must therefore beware of treating this truth differently from others. We do not suspend belief in the Trinity or Christ's substitutionary death until all our questions have been answered. 'Our confidence in the New Testament as a doctrinal guide is so grounded in unassailable and compelling evidence, that we believe its teachings despite the difficulties which they raise . . . We may on the same compelling evidence accept, in full confidence, the teaching of the same Scripture as to the nature of its own inspiration, prior to a full understanding of how all the phenomena of Scripture are to be adjusted to it.'[4]

One last query about the Bible's full reliability requires comment : some allege that this whole position is falsified because it is an argument in a circle. It is logical enough, granted the initial premise; but is not the initial premise also what you are trying to prove? Is this therefore an attempt to prove the Bible (to be inspired and infallible) from the Bible? Now there is a real measure of truth in this, as will become evident when certain facts are recalled. In chapter 2 we saw that God cannot be 'proved'. While there is massive evidence for His existence, God is in fact His own proof. He authenticates Himself.

The case is parallel with God's Word. There is similarly massive evidence to confirm that the Bible is God's Word and to show that belief in it is supremely rational: for example, the unity of the Bible through all its sixty-six books and the fulfilment of prophecy. But we cannot

[4] B. B. Warfield, op. cit., p. 216.

'prove' the Bible to be God's Word; God in His Word is His own authentication. The inner witness of the Spirit of God bears testimony to us that the Bible is His work.

'To attempt to demonstrate the authority of Scripture as the Word of God by reason or tradition or probability is not only a vain occupation but subversive of the very authority claimed for Scripture, for then human judgment, in the form of reason, tradition, probability, and so on, is set up as an authority superior to that of divine revelation, to which the latter must submit. To do this is in effect to deny the supremacy of Holy Scripture as the Word of God. This does not mean, however, that the Christian is invited to take a leap in the dark where the Bible is concerned – on the contrary, for, firstly, Scripture, as God's revelation, is clear and luminous and self-authenticating, and secondly, the believer has an entirely adequate and conclusive witness to Scripture as the authoritative revelation of God in the Holy Spirit who confirms it is the Word of God to his heart. The internal testimony of the Holy Spirit, which the Reformers stressed, is conclusive, and it is at the same time a testimony that is objective (as being that of the Holy Spirit) and subjective (as being within the believer's own heart).'[5]

It is quite false therefore to think that 'proving the Bible by the Bible' discredits the whole procedure and its conclusions. If the Bible were merely a human book, this would be so; but if it is from God, we must go to God speaking there for the truth He reveals. Moreover, this is involved in following Christ. Christ received His Bible as the Word of God, His Father. To be a disciple of Christ means learning and accepting His attitude to Scripture, and therefore going to it for all our knowledge about God. It is out of obedience to Christ that we must go to the

[5] P. E. Hughes, *Scripture and Myth*, p. 29.

Bible for its teaching about all divine matters, its own nature included.

We believe that allegiance to Christ coincides precisely with the facts of revelation and inspiration; and that all these factors compel us gladly to put our full confidence in the infallible truth of Holy Scripture.

CHAPTER TEN

A QUESTION OF AUTHORITY

TO MANY, more perhaps than we think, this universe is bewildering and impersonal. They sense themselves to be at sea, drifting without chart or compass or captain. Despite their knowledge and sophistication, they lack certainty. They hold great hopes, but are more familiar with despair. They may have their own standards, but yet are not sure that they do right.

We think of such being outside organized Christianity and in the main they may be. This is why we seek to present Christ to them; He is the only foundation on which anyone can build enduringly, His Word the only truth on which anyone can rely unshakably. But the questions of authority and certainty are pressing within the ranks of professing Christians also. Does authority lie in church and tradition, in reason or feeling, or in Scripture? These are the options usually presented to us and, as a matter of plain fact, all Christians live by the authority of one of these.

Some think that, by consulting all three, they can get the best of all worlds. But what happens when their teaching conflicts? We seem to be involved in a three-sided contest : church-tradition *versus* reason-feeling *versus* the Bible. Take the question of atonement as an example to show the dilemma. The Bible declares that Christ alone dealt once for all with human sin in His death; the 'church' may teach that in the mass the work of our redemption is carried on and that Mary is to be invoked as Mediatrix[1]; my religious feeling may rule out an objective atonement altogether. Which view is authoritative? Since they cannot all be right, the issue of authority becomes a matter of selecting the most viable of the contenders. In practice this is what happens: we cannot avoid giving one precedence over the others when decisions have to be made.

As far as it goes, this is certainly true. But is it the right way of framing the question? The approach we have described above is an attempt to face the question: *'What is our authority? Is it the Bible, or the church, or my reason?'* Now this makes the issue rather impersonal; our task is one which can become quite academic (where to locate authority). We believe that the proper question with which to begin is this: *'Who has authority?'* To this question there is only one answer: God. God alone has the right to rule. For anyone or anything to usurp His kingship is the most brazen insult to Him. When therefore we are thinking about the problem of authority for ourselves individually or for the church, we are thinking about the personal rule of the living God over us. The question of authority is the question of our submission to God Himself. This does not avoid the church *v.* reason *v.* Bible issue, as we shall see; but it does put it in a different light. The questions we now ask are these: How does God exercise His personal authority? Where does God speak? How may His voice (not men's or mine) be heard?

To some it seems a sufficient, self-evident answer to these questions to reply that God's authority is expressed in His Son. Did not the Father say of Him: 'This is my beloved Son; listen to him' (Mk. 9:7)? Is He not 'head over all things for the church' (Eph. 1:22)? But the

[1] *Cf. The Documents of Vatican II*, edited by Walter M. Abbott, pp. 16, 91, 141, 535.

questions remain : How may Christ's authentic voice be heard? Where does He really speak? Which Christ am I to follow? This is no side issue. Do I follow the 'Christ' of my own mind or others' imagining, the 'Christ' of some tradition, or the Christ of the Bible? As F. A. Schaeffer has written, 'Christians need to notice, at this point, that the Reformation said "Scripture Alone" and not "the Revelation of God in Christ Alone". If you do not have the view of the Scriptures that the Reformers had, you really have no content in the word "Christ" — and this is the modern drift in theology. Modern theology uses the word without content because "Christ" is cut away from the Scriptures.'[2] There are many mutually exclusive views of Christ; they cannot all be true.

So the question comes back to this : How has God made His personal authority known? Where and through what does *He* speak? To put the question in this personal way is at once to begin to clarify it, for we can see how it applies to the sources of authority suggested.

First, the authority of human reason or feeling. God is God, not man. I am not God. God is not an idea in my mind, the fabrication of my wishful thinking, a psychologically useful device to assuage my anxieties. How then can my religious feeling or reason be God's authoritative voice? Can anything in me, a mortal and a sinner, carry absolute divine authority?

Second, the authority of the 'church'. How can any traditions be God's authoritative voice to overrule Scripture? We need to recall three facts. For one thing, there is no unanimity about what tradition teaches, nor can there be. Any unity of tradition is either imaginary or else artificially imposed by the 'church'. For another, all true traditions were incorporated into the New Testament canon, all untrue traditions excluded. To believe in a

[2] F. A. Schaeffer, *Escape from Reason*, p. 20.

perpetuated tradition with authority over Scripture is to ignore the very reasons which led the apostles to form the New Testament. In the third place, the gospel is prior to the church. This priority is, as a matter of verifiable historical fact, a chronological one : God created the church by means of the gospel and goes on creating it, that is, adding to it, by the same good news. This priority is also of necessity a logical and theological one, since the church always depends on the gospel for its life and continuance. Where the gospel is neglected or denied, a church ceases to be a true congregation of God. No 'church' may claim authority to deny or add to the biblical gospel, which brought it into being and keeps it in being.

What we have said does not deny that much can be learnt through Christian experience or tradition. The Christian who knows nothing of that enlightenment which God has given to Christians individually and corporately in the past is much impoverished in his understanding and devotion. But the question we are pursuing is not whether these other sources may prove helpful to Christian life; it is simply the question of how we may hear God's personal, living and authoritative voice. Only one reply to this is consistent with God's being and deeds : that God speaks with authority in and through Scripture. If the other alleged sources of authority speak what is true, it is because they are accurately reflecting Scripture or applying it to particular topics.

Scripture alone has authority, not as a mere book but as God's voice. Scripture is not speculation, as is man's thought or emotion; it is revelation. Scripture is not errant or at odds within itself, as is tradition; it is God's infallible truth. As the Old Testament was to Christ the authoritative voice of His Father, so the whole Scripture is to us. By its nature it cannot be otherwise. Scripture is the supreme authority; it is indeed the sole authority, for it alone is the pure Word of God.

This makes the profoundest difference to our approach to the Bible. With other books we reserve our right to question the writer and reject what he says. Not so here. This is no ordinary literature, for to criticize the Bible (in the sense of sitting in judgment over what it teaches) is to criticize God. Are we to censure Him? Are we to suggest that He should have spoken otherwise? What pathetic presumption that would be. In fact the positions are reversed, for all the rights are God's. He has, and through Scripture exercises, the right to criticize our lives and reject our ideas.

This does not mean that we must be passive and unthinking. The Christian who never reads serious Christian books, who rarely thinks about his faith and only occasionally studies Scripture, is a scandal and affront to the God who gave him his mind. That needs to be underlined. It is not for us to stand over God's Word, but to sit under it. It corrects us, and not the reverse. When God speaks it is our place to use our minds to understand, receive and apply His word. It is exacting mentally to work at Scripture so that, with the Spirit's help, it yields up more and more of its riches. But we owe it to God, who gave us the Bible, to concentrate all our powers of thought on grasping all that He has revealed.

The Bible is thus the expression and instrument of God's personal sovereignty. It is the sceptre by which He rules in His church and world. As such it is final and unique.

AUTHORITATIVE – IN WHAT?

In what spheres is the Bible authoritative? To this we must give the same reply as we did for its infallible truth.

It is authoritative in everything about which it purports to convey God's mind to us. This is often defined as 'all matters of faith and conduct'. Rightly understood, this is true; but how should we understand it? Some take these matters as merely being a list of, say, ten major doctrines and ten rules of behaviour. They seem to suppose that they have submitted fully to the authority of God in Scripture if they subscribe to the major tenets (the deity of Christ, His substitutionary death, *etc.*) and accept the moral injunctions (to be kind, honest, *etc.*). Such an outlook essentially maintains that the Bible is our guide for 'religious' questions, but not for 'secular'. It asserts that the Bible does not deal with many matters of modern life.

As we have already shown, it is no secret that the Bible does not teach about internal combustion engines or tell me the correct gap for my sparking plugs. But is the Bible just our rule in 'spiritual' matters? To this, we suggest, the answer is an emphatic No. The Bible *is* about the whole of life – and therefore is our authority for it all. The way in which we can demonstrate this is simply to pose the question : of what does life essentially consist? Life is more than bare existence; what is its central characteristic? The Bible answers that life is composed of relationships. It suggests this to us by the simple fact that it is all about relationships itself. There is the relationship between Father, Son and Holy Spirit in the Godhead. We are told of God's relationship to His creation, His creatures, their history and actions, their sin and guilt, their dignity and destiny; of His concern for individuals and His church through Christ. Men's relationship with God comes under review : their attitude to His world, His gifts, His Son, His Word; their relationship to money, time, the state, other people. In this sense the Bible educates us in (and is authoritative for) everything from profound philosophical issues to problems of everyday conduct. God in Scripture speaks to individuals about every branch of their thought and activity.

On this basis it is quite wrong to confine God's voice in Scripture to distinctively religious topics and allow ourselves autonomy in the 'secular' sphere. The Bible indeed permits no such absolute distinction to be drawn; after all, what is the supposedly secular sphere but part of God's one world? We are now in a position to illustrate briefly how the authority of the Bible as God's voice enters and claims every aspect of our existence.

Individuals and the church. Both personal and corporate matters are covered. The Bible deals with my relationship to God; my dealing with temptation, neighbours, colleagues, circumstances, bereavement, doubt, success. It is God's lucid instruction for my ambitions, values, thoughts; for the use of my body, my home, my leisure. Equally the Bible teaches about our corporate life, both in the nation and community where I live and also within the body of Christ. It offers a clear picture of the life and order of the church, its message, ministry, organization, discipline, worship.

Time and eternity. The Bible talks about both temporal and eternal questions. God gives counsel about issues which are only for the here and now, *e.g.* marriage, the family, the state, the church's ministry, temptation. It talks about our attitude to daily work and establishes the dignity of all that is done to and for God in this age. At the same time it covers issues which are eternal : our inheritance and future glory in Christ, the fact of resurrection and judgment.

Conduct and thought. The Bible covers practical and theoretical, moral and intellectual issues. It holds out God's wisdom to me concerning possessions, time, talents, tongue, family. It speaks of how I should regard those who love me, hate me, employ me, depend on me. It gears abiding principles and objectives to practical moral issues.

It also determines my approach to theoretical issues and to the study of the various branches of knowledge. It shapes my mind as I approach individual disciplines, for example questions raised in philosophy, physics, psychology, theology, education. It does not answer all 'how?' questions (how does my car work? how does the brain function? how should I construct an experiment in chemistry or sociology?). What it does do essentially is to give the presuppositions and framework with which to approach such disciplines. A few examples may illustrate this.

To the Christian in education it says that all his theories and practice must be built on the basis of what God has revealed men to be and not, for example, on the hypothesis of the inherent goodness of human nature. To the Christian in psychiatry the Bible speaks of the fact that man is more than animal, more than machine; and so it rules out schools of thought which would claim to explain man *solely* in behaviouristic or mechanistic terms. To the Christian in philosophy it warns that man's mind is not autonomous; the philosopher must begin from what God has revealed about Himself, the universe and men. To the Christian studying comparative religion the Bible displays what God has said about general revelation and man's sin; it excludes all theories that other religions are stages on some universal road to God and advises that they are more the result of human blindness than examples of man's enlightenment. To the Christian in the natural sciences it underscores (as it did to the originators of modern science) the fact that he is studying God's creation; it alerts him to the impossibility of neutrality to God in the world He has made and makes him sensitive to the denial of God which is latent in some theories. To the Christian ap-

97

proaching the arts, it quickens his appreciation of beauty and creativity; and at the same time awakens him to a true outlook on God, man and values.

In all disciplines the Christian will look for the presuppositions on which any theories or views of life are founded. He is aware that in every sphere of knowledge man is faced with evidence of God and examples of His work (even though men do not recognize the fact); he tries to perceive both how this comes out in the thinking of others and how it should mould his mind on the same issues. He accepts that all man's study in and of a world that is God's cannot but be affected radically by man's relationship to Him. There are no spheres of human activity which are independent of God; all are affected by what God has made known.

The Bible also gives the Christian an over-all perspective, a 'world-view'. It shows him that there is a coherence and inter-connection between all the disciplines. If it is scholarship to know the facts of a particular subject and be able to use them, it is wisdom to perceive the relationship between different areas of experience and knowledge. When the Bible sets all our life and thought, our actions and motives, our investigations and our creativity under the fact of God's Lordship and in the setting of His world, it teaches us how to view things as a coherent whole. 'Today we have a weakness in our educational process in failing to understand the natural associations between the disciplines. We tend to study all our disciplines in unrelated parallel lines. This tends to be true in both Christian and secular education. This is one of the reasons why evangelical Christians have been taken by surprise at the tremendous shift that has come in our generation. We have studied our exegesis as exegesis, our theology as theology, our philosophy as philosophy; we study something about art as art; we study music as music, without understanding that these are the things of man, and the things of man are not unrelated parallel lines.'[3]

In ways such as these God speaks in the Bible with authority for our entire living. And as a result we are bound to submit to God so speaking. We use 'bound' advisedly; this *is* a bondage. Every thought is to be brought into captivity to Christ. We are to obey Him as much in the spheres of intellectual pursuit as in those of morals or the emotions. But, and this is a most crucial qualification, to the Christian this is an infinitely welcome bondage. So welcome is it that he does not conceive of it as restrictive at all. It spells release from his otherwise petty, puny, earth-bound thoughts. It opens his mind to the height and breadth and length and depth of God's self-disclosure in Christ. It gives him eyes to see the graciousness and glory of God's creative and re-creative work. It liberates him to enjoy God's gifts as favours and use them to the full. It exhilarates him to begin in this way to enter into God's purposes for him and others and this world.

This is a bondage, but only a bondage to the God of grace whom the Christian loves because He first loved and spoke to him. This is God's glorious, emancipating purpose in giving us His authoritative Word : that our human minds should think His divine thoughts after Him; that our sinful hearts should be fired by His saving and renewing truth; that our disfigured lives should come to reflect something of His glory. This bondage is perfect freedom.

[3] F. A. Schaeffer, *op. cit.*, p. 12.

CHAPTER ELEVEN

GETTING THE MESSAGE

THE BIBLE has no introductory chapter on 'rules of interpretation' (though some have attempted to rectify this omission!). How then may we get the Bible's message? Should we just trust the Spirit to 'lead us into all truth' and forget about rules? Are there indeed any objective principles to guide our understanding? Is one set of rules as valid as another?

This is a burning issue – unless we are to be for ever content with the great divergence among professing Christians on many issues. We must not exaggerate this difficulty, for among those who receive the authority of the Bible there is impressive agreement on basic issues. But the difficulty is there and some, of course, have their own explanation of divergent views : 'All the world's queer except me and thee . . . and I'm not so sure about thee'; or the proud mother watching the army parade who declared: 'Look, they're all out of step except my Johnny!'

IT IS ALL SO CLEAR . . .

This is not so far removed from reality as might appear. Certainly many unorthodox groups do this. To Mormons, for example, it is self-evident that Ezekiel 37 : 15–20 proves that the Bible itself expects and inculcates the need for the Book of Mormon. That passage speaks of two sticks, which Ezekiel is first to label (the one 'for the House of

Judah', the other 'for the House of Joseph') and then to join. According to Mormon doctrine, the first is the Bible, the second the Book of Mormon . . . and both are to be joined. It is so neat and obvious . . . until you read the whole passage, at least down to verse 23. Then you discover very quickly that the sticks stand for the southern and northern kingdoms, and not for books at all.

Earnest Christians are not exempt from this either. Some are totally persuaded of certain teaching on prophecy. Various Old Testament passages are, to them, obvious proof of such views. It never seems to occur to them to ask what they are doing when they take details out of such highly symbolic passages and give them such a literalistic meaning.

. . . OR IS IT?

Others, rejecting the bulldozing simplicity of such an approach, urge that it is 'all a matter of interpretation'. To them truth in Scripture is very far from self-evident. Nothing seems clearer than that the Bible is often indistinct and ambiguous. Because of this none can be sure that his interpretation is right, and therefore no view can be ruled out. I have a right to believe what I think is clear, but no right to say that what you hold is erroneous. I must make room for ambiguity. While I do not have to subscribe to your notions, I must accept them as a valid Christian alternative simply because the Bible is not perspicuous. Perhaps in time we may come to a larger view of truth; at the moment we cannot be firm or definite.

Now we may have overdrawn these two approaches. But what are we to make of them? The first, though often utterly wrong in its application, is not so wide of the mark in principle. It may draw the line in the wrong place, on the wrong basis and in an unloving spirit; but at least it recognizes that truth is distinguishable from error. Truth is no synthesis of every opinion; not every view is equally valid; truth has limits and error lies beyond them.

The second position must be faulted in principle. It urges that God's self-disclosure is not clear; by innuendo therefore it charges God with having given a revelation which is not revealing. If God has spoken at all, He has apparently done so without letting anyone clearly hear His voice. But is the Bible really so imprecise and vague? It would, to say the least, be strange if God, having given a revelation, should have left us devoid of any sure means of arriving at its content. This would be quite inconsistent with the nature and works of God as shown in the Bible.

Christian experience certainly demonstrates that Scripture has proved transparent enough for the simplest Christian to live by. Those whom the Spirit has brought to new life do find God's Word a lamp to their feet and a light to their path. William Tyndale was right when he believed that a ploughboy with the Bible would know more of God than the most learned ecclesiastic who ignored it. How else can we explain the fact that through the Bible the Spirit has brought people throughout the world to know, love and serve God – people of all cultures and languages, of every intellect and temperament?

At the lowest estimate, Scripture is unambiguous about the gospel. There is no equivocation about this truth : that the holy God in grace acquits guilty sinners solely through their faith in Christ and on the basis of Christ's death in their place. Indeed, many critics of the Bible have given unintended but significant testimony to the clarity of its message. An example of this concerns the birth narratives of our Lord. Luke 1 : 5 – 2 : 52 patently affirms the virgin birth of Christ. The fact that it is unmistakably present in the passage poses a problem for those disinclined to accept the doctrine of the virgin birth itself. 'It is perfectly true, they say, . . . that an attestation of the virgin birth now stands in that narrative; but, they say, that attestation of the virgin birth formed no part of the original narrative, but came into it by interpolation.'[1] When such critics argue that the Bible is mistaken at a given point, they are tacitly admitting that what it actually teaches is clear. The dilemma is no longer one of interpretation, for the sense is patent; the problem moves over into the area of authority – whether men will go by their wisdom or God's revelation, whether they (as in this example) will accept the supernatural or not.

THE BIBLE'S OWN GUIDELINES

Our enquiry now, however, is how we are to get further into the Bible's meaning. If it is by discovering and applying right principles of interpretation, what are they? We do not have space here to do more than outline the main principles, let alone illustrate them. In any case, these have been well set out and exemplified by A. M. Stibbs; his book *Understanding God's Word* is a natural sequel to this. Rather than cover that ground again, I want here to tackle a rather different question.

Principles of interpretation often appear to be the arbitrary, personal choice of the individual concerned. How then do we arrive at right principles of understanding the Bible? How can we justify them? How may we be sure that they have objective validity? I propose to offer some basic rules and then in each case to try to answer the question : why should we work by this rule? In other words I want to show that certain guidelines for understanding the Bible arise directly and necessarily from its nature. They are not arbitrary, nor are they the property of any particular school of interpretation. The Bible itself presses

[1] J. Gresham Machen, *The Virgin Birth of Christ*, p. 119.

these upon us and does not leave us to grope by ourselves. What are these signposts?

Get to the text

Paul said that all Scripture was 'breathed out' by God. If we were able to press him about what he was referring to, he would surely say that he was talking about Scripture as God gave it. That is, he was not speaking about copies or translations. Now while we do not have the originals, God's amazing care of the copying and transmission of manuscripts has ensured that we are not at a loss because of this. This means that we must begin by getting at the text of Scripture. Why? In order to get as near as possible to Scripture 'as originally given'. For this, if we do not know Hebrew or Greek, we must use the best translation(s). Paraphrases or looser renderings may throw light, for example, on the current application of a passage, but because they are a stage further away from the original they cannot consistently help in this essential first stage. A strong case may be made for holding to that translation which seems most satisfactory; at least we can then get to know its strengths and weaknesses over the years and so get closer to the original.

Study the original meaning

Why? Because the Bible is not a series of bare propositions. Its component books were written at different places and in contrasting periods of history. Many were directed to a distinct group of people with their own set of problems in the first instance. The Bible is written in words which conveyed (or were made to convey) precise shades of meaning to their first readers. It was given in Hebrew and Greek cultural settings.

This does not mean that we cannot understand the book unless we make ourselves expert in such matters as

Ancient Near Eastern geography, politics and archaeology, though such knowledge can help. It does mean
that we should try to put ourselves in the position of the
original readers. The Bible consists of words : each is important, though the meaning of words can change. We
must never put a meaning on a word which it could not
have held originally and must always ask : what did the
words convey at the time? Again, the Bible is packed
with illustrations, figures of speech, idioms : what do they
tell us of the people's life and background? What ideas
were being conveyed then? Further, the Bible was not
given all at once or with our chapter and verse divi-
sions : how then would the first hearers have understood
the part they had? In the New Testament are many allusions to the Old; since many of the first converts were
well versed in the Old Testament, how would this have
helped them to grasp the New? What Old Testament
truths lie behind New Testament teaching?

Look for the enduring message

To see what the original readers read out of a passage is
only a beginning. The next question is 'how may we discern the abiding sense of Scripture?' If these things 'were
written down for our instruction', how may we receive
that education from Scripture? Some principles stand out
from the Bible :

(a) *Let the Bible explain itself.* Why? Because Scripture is a unity. Through the many writers appears the
single mind of God. We should start from this fact. If I
come to what seems to me to be a disagreement between
the writers, I should suspect my understanding rather
than their harmony. Rather than dispense with one to
retain the other, I should look elsewhere in Scripture for
light on the perplexity. God's revelation may be supra-

rational; it is not anti-rational. Therefore let Scripture in this way disclose its wholeness and coherence.

(b) *Remember the purpose of the Bible.* Initially remember its ultimate purpose. Why? First because this will save us from far-fetched or fanciful interpretations. Some people have taken Leviticus 17 : 11 ('the life of the flesh is in the blood') as teaching about the function of the blood-stream. Dr Christiaan Barnard alleged in a television discussion that the Bible spoke of (physical) heart transplantation when it said in Ezekiel 36 : 26 : 'I will take out of your flesh the heart of stone and give you a heart of flesh.' (By the same interpretative token, it should have been God who did the surgery and the heart removed should have been a literal piece of stone !) The Bible is for saving truth, not medical or similar know-how.

Second, remember the purpose of each individual part of the Bible. Why? Take one familiar problem as an example. Many have been perplexed by the apparent conflict between Paul and James on justification. So we need to ask : what is the purpose of James' letter and of Paul's to the Galatians? Paul is writing about the way of justification (through faith alone). James is concerned, in a complementary way, about the evidence or expression of that faith which justifies (faith issuing in obedience). To see their purpose is to see their concord.

(c) *Examine the context.* Remember the old jibe hurled at some preachers : 'A text without a context is a pretext'. Why is this relevant? Because God has set each text in a context. He did not give us the Bible in the form of a selection of verses for devotional use. Luther wrote disdainfully of those who try to establish their arguments on individual words or verses, while ignoring the contexts. It is their way, he said, 'to hold the text in sovereign contempt, and to concern themselves merely with picking out a word, torturing it with their figures and nailing it to the cross of their own chosen meaning in utter disregard of the surrounding context, of what comes before and after, and of the author's aim and intention.'[2]

An example of this is a common use of Isaiah 30 : 15 : 'In returning and rest you shall be saved; in quietness and in trust shall be your strength.' Some take this as though it were an injunction to slip away into the peace of a country garden or the solitude of an empty church. 'One is nearer God's heart in a garden' would seem to say roughly the same thing! This transforms the verse into a piece of useful psycho-therapy. But what is the context? It is a sobering one; God's people have ceased to rely on Him, have gone (against His explicit will) to find help from the Egyptians against the invading Assyrian army, and have begged God's spokesmen to stop speaking about Him. As these storm clouds of disobedience were building up into judgment, God said to them, 'in returning and rest . . . in quietness and in trust . . .' This is God's strong and solemn command to them to turn from self-confidence and disobedience and put their whole trust in Him and His power.

To see a text in its context may rule out what we would like to think the passage says; but it invariably yields a deeper and more satisfying sense.

(d) *Move from the light to the dark*. Go from what you have understood to what you have not yet fathomed. Why? Partly because we have an uncanny penchant for starting with 'problem' verses, as the questions submitted to most Christian brains-trusts bear out. If the 'brains' suggest that we should start from clearer passages, this is taken as evading the issue. But is it? Not necessarily. We should start from the known simply because we cannot grasp all the Bible at once. Our appreciation of it is but partial and it can only increase as we take what is clearest

[2] Martin Luther, *The Bondage of the Will*.

and proceed from there into what (to us) is still in shadow.
That then becomes clearer and forms the basis for an ever-
deepening grasp of God's truth.

One illustration of this arises from what Hebrews
6 : 4–6 seems to say about Christians 'falling away'. Space
permits us only to outline an approach to such difficulties. First we must look at *the background of the passage.*
Hebrews is obviously steeped in Old Testament ideas and
language. Indeed the controversial phrases in Hebrews 6
(mentioned below) have the ring of the language of the
exodus. Scripture often uses such analogies or pictures –
think of Christ's great 'I am' sayings. Clearly Christ did
not intend that every imaginable feature of a door or a
vine should be pressed to yield up truth about Himself.
And here we should not press the details of the exodus too
literally either.

Second we must find out *the true sense of that passage*;
for example, what do such phrases as these really mean :
'enlightened,' 'tasted the heavenly gift', 'partakers of the
Holy Spirit', 'tasted the goodness of the word of God and
the powers of the age to come'? Do these necessarily mean
that those spoken of were regenerate? Does it say so? Was
the writer describing actual people, those to whom he
wrote (see verses 9–12)? How do the above phrases fit with
others in the same passage, such as 'the full assurance of
hope until the end' or 'those who inherit the promises'?

Third, we must bring to bear *the teaching of other
parts of Scripture* relating to apostasy and endurance. If
these are found to be unequivocal, we shall come back to
this passage to see whether we have read it correctly. We
shall look again at the purpose of the writer of Hebrews;
whether he is speaking hypothetically; and whether he is
thinking of Christians as they appear to be (by their outward profession) or as they are known to God (by their

inward state of heart). In this way we can begin to see light on the darker places.

(e) *Look at the type of literature.* Why? Because the Bible is composed of different types of literature. God gave some of it as prose, other parts as poetry, allegory, parable, apocalyptic, prophecy, *etc*. We are not meant to take poetic imagery in a stultifying literalistic manner. We are not intended to press every detail in a parable for spiritual significance, as though (and we have heard this solemnly propounded) the ring placed on the prodigal's finger pictured everlasting life ... because the ring had no end! Some evangelicals have failed to see the literary character of Scripture and have treated it like a railway timetable; some liberals have so stressed the literary forms that they have overlooked the substance which those forms were meant to convey.

(f) *Understand the unity of the Old and New Testaments.* The Old anticipates Christ's coming. It gives promises, shadows of the coming realities, types of the expected fulfilment, pre-dawn light. God could, we may suppose, have given the whole Bible at the time of Abraham or Moses, or delayed it all until Paul's day. Instead He gave it part by part progressively. This explains why there is so frequent reference to purely physical factors in the Old Testament prophets – the exodus from Egypt, the promised land, the temple, Jerusalem, the throne of David. If God had spoken in directly spiritual terms of spiritual blessing to follow, no-one would then have comprehended a word of it. But in this way God spoke of spiritual covenant benefits in anticipation of the promised Mediator. What then are we to make of this Old Testament language? Should we find pictures of Christ in every item of the tabernacle furniture or every incident in Israel's history? Should we take all its prophecy in a way that would seem to make God more concerned about so many square miles of ground in the Middle East than about anything else?

We might be left to do this if we had only the Old Testament. But, in God's providence, we have the New. As this looks back on Christ's first coming we find there the full light of the 'Dayspring from on high'; the promises and shadows are illuminated by their realization in Christ and His body, the church. The New Testament thus gives us guidance concerning what to read out of the Old and what not to read into it. If we make it a rule not to spiritualize or allegorize the Old Testament without warrant or example from the New, we shall not go astray.

To take an example, the New Testament does not take the story of Abraham's willingness to sacrifice Isaac as a type of Christ. This is surprising, since the story lends numerous analogies to the work of redemption : the father offering his only son given him by promise; the son going willingly in obedience; the infinite cost to the father; *etc.* We think that 'God will provide himself the lamb' (Gn. 22 :8) must speak of Christ. But in the Old Testament this stands as an example of the willing obedience of faith; the New Testament does not add to that, and neither should we. Indeed we might well miss the thrust concerning obedience in our anxiety to read Christ into the passage. When all is said and done, there are many other Old Testament passages which the New Testament endorses as setting Christ forth.

In such ways the Bible dictates to us the ways in which it should be interpreted. It offers us principles which, because they emerge from the character of the Bible itself, may be consistently applied throughout. For this very reason they help to free those who follow them from mere subjectivism. Difficulties of interpretation still persist, of course, though many of these are more imaginary than real because based on antipathy to what the Bible says.

Other difficulties arise because Christians have not thought about the principles which unconsciously govern their approach to Scripture; if once they had to describe their unwitting working rules, they would immediately revise them.

THE HUMAN FACTOR

We do not pretend, ostrich-like, that even the remaining variant views are insignificant. Differences about God's sovereignty and human responsibility, millennialism, spiritual gifts, episcopacy and independency, baptism – these and others have a profound effect on the life of the church and cannot be ignored. But does this mean that the Bible is not clearly expressed? There is another way of looking at this; it starts with the fact that the Bible presents itself to us as God's revelation, understandable and unmistakable. Start there and the question is not 'Why isn't the Bible clear?' but 'Why do we not perceive its message more clearly?' The finger of suspicion is pointing at us, and this is as it should be. What factors therefore *in us* hinder us from seeing clearly what God has displayed?

Background and tradition

Obviously these predispose us for or against certain views. In consequence we all tend to start with certain conclusions and interpret Scripture to support these. This does not mean that we should jettison what our background gave us or accept it merely because of how it came to us. The crucial point is whether it is true, not whence or through whom it came.

Pattern thinking

Scripture itself, because it is a unity created by the one God, contains a definite pattern of teaching. All its parts are components of one body of truth. But we must beware of starting or finishing with the wrong pattern. J. S. Wright illustrated this from Jehovah's Witnesses and Christian Scientists. 'If we start with the fixed idea that the unity of the Godhead means a bare mathematical unity, and that divine Sonship inevitably means that the Father existed before the Son, Scripture then cannot be clear to us, since we have tried to fit it into an arbitrary pattern of thinking ... To give a further example, Christian Science starts with a radical dualism between spirit and matter, so that God cannot have created matter.'[3]

We need to examine ourselves about this. Thinking according to an unbiblical pattern may pre-close our eyes to what Scripture plainly exhibits for all who have eyes to see. We see this fault in others; that is why they get heated in discussion. But are they alone guilty? When we are merely trying to defend a position, and especially when we sense our argument to be weak, we all tend to get heated. So when you next feel your mental temperature to be rising, ask yourself : am *I* starting from the wrong pattern of thought?

Wilful blindness

Perhaps the most serious barrier is pride, our aversion as sinners to God's truth and our hatred of climbing down from defended positions. Have we not all known times when we knew full well what the Bible said, but found it too costly or irksome or humbling? Have we not all been familiar with the inward awareness that the other person's conviction, not our own, coincided with God's truth? So we produced a different interpretation and tried to make it look plausible ... or made out that the Bible was not lucid after all.

[3] 'The Perspicuity of Scripture', *Theological Students' Fellowship Bulletin* (Summer 1959), p. 7.

It is the work of the Holy Spirit, having brought us to see and love Scripture as the Word of our Saviour, to enable our minds increasingly to comprehend it and our wills to obey it. In the very constitution of this book He has incorporated the principles of correct interpretation. He now works in our minds and hearts to make clear *to us* what is already objectively clear in His revelation. He is working to remove our bias and prejudice against His truth and enlighten our minds to appreciate it. Once we were darkened in our understanding. The light of God's unveiled truth was there, but we could not perceive it. Now by the Holy Spirit we are being renewed in the spirit of our minds to see more and more of God in His Word (Eph. 4:18, 23). And this must go on until we see Him and know Him as He knows us.

Who can tell how much we would grow in the knowledge and love of God if only we obeyed what is already clear to us in Scripture?

CHAPTER TWELVE

TOWARDS A BIBLICAL MIND

GOD IS DOING something dramatic in every Christian. He is promoting a total inward revolution.

When completed, this will be a phenomenal transformation. If you doubt it, stop and recall how you used to think and live as a non-Christian. You were everything and God nothing. You came first, others last and God nowhere. God never seriously affected your views about money or sex, science or art, your values or your neighbours; or if He did, it was merely to salve your conscience and make you feel better. You were not aware of all this; but looking back you can see how self-regarding your outlook was. Life was you; you were the centre of your little world.

One day, however, self-regard will be gone and God will be everything. One day God is going to be as exclusively your life as you once were. This will be God's achievement. He has undertaken to do this. He is working at it in us now, so that our desires and deeds may please Him (Phil. 2:13). He triggered off this revolution in us and He will bring it to completion at the day of Christ (Phil. 1:6).

But how is He bringing this revolution about? How did He change me from what I was? How is He transforming me from what I am? Scripture replies unequivocally to these questions: God the Holy Spirit works through His Word.

It was by this Word that the Holy Spirit gave us new

life and saving faith. 'Faith comes from what is heard, and what is heard comes by the preaching of Christ' (Rom. 10:17). 'You have been born anew ... through the living and abiding word of God' (1 Pet. 1:23). His Word may have reached us through public preaching or private Bible reading; through a Christian biography or recollecting some long forgotten truth; but however it came, it was God's Word that gave life. Of course, God works in many ways. He helps us, for example, through other Christians or the circumstances He orders. But other Christians give genuine help only as they reflect Scripture and remind us of it; circumstances help us forward only as we understand them in the light of the Bible. The Word of God is crucial.

This is why God gave the Bible: 'All scripture is inspired by God and profitable for teaching, for reproof, for correction, and for training in righteousness, *that the man of God may be complete, equipped for every good work*' (2 Tim. 3:16, 17). Paul says: 'Let the word of Christ dwell in you richly'; then you may 'do everything in the name of the Lord Jesus' (Col. 3:16, 17).

God's Word is the instrument by which God's Spirit transforms the Christian. This was how John Bunyan became such a great man of God. 'Prick him anywhere and you will find that his blood is bibline; the very essence of the Bible flows through him.' The same thing stands out in the life of a modern Christian martyr, Jim Elliot. He was killed in 1956 in Ecuador by Auca tribespeople to whom he was seeking to take the gospel. How was he so devoted to Christ and this enterprise? His wife wrote: 'It was Marcus Aurelius who said, "A man's thoughts dye his soul." Constant dwelling on the words of the Lord dyed Jim's soul.'[1]

[1] Elizabeth Elliot, *Shadow of the Almighty*, p. 52.

CHANGE YOUR MIND?

This fact has one very obvious implication, so obvious that we are often oblivious to it. It is this: that God changes us by changing our minds. This is His method: 'Be transformed by the renewal of your mind' (Rom. 12:2). God is concerned to expel from our minds all self-centred concepts and aims. He is purging our minds of what sullies and darkens them, and filling them with what purifies and gives light. He purposes the full renewing of our minds. This puts the challenge to us: we cannot be satisfied with less than a biblical mind, the mind of Christ.

Now God is not concerned merely with our minds. His book affects our will, affections, emotions, conscience and memory; our speech, conduct and relationships. Yet the Bible is a book. A book is to be read. And reading, whatever response it may lead to, is primarily a mental exercise. God has favoured us with His autobiography in order that we might know and think His thoughts in every department of our lives. What He has said is to form our outlook, whether about the Trinity or temptation, about the Messiah or money, about grace or guidance. The Bible is not meant to produce some emotional, non-rational experience. Basically God has addressed it to our minds.

This does not mean that we can grasp the import of Scripture apart from the Holy Spirit. We constantly depend on His enlightenment. But that in no way reduces the significance of our minds. Paul connected our responsibility to think with God's promise to give understanding. Writing to Timothy he said: 'Think over what I say, for the Lord will grant you understanding in everything.' Timothy was therefore to study or do his best to present himself to God as one approved, rightly handling the word of truth (2 Tim. 2 : 7, 15).

To some this may seem to be making faith a purely intellectual exercise. Nothing could be further from the truth. We are not advocating that Christians should simply cram their brains with theological data. As John Newton wrote, we are to read Scripture 'not as an attorney may read a will, merely to know the sense; but as the heir reads it, as a description and proof of his interest.'[2] Moreover, hearers must always be doers; the point is that we can never be doers if we are not hearers. James' warning against being mere hearers (1 : 22) is echoed by Paul writing to the Corinthians. Six times within one chapter he asks : 'Do you not know . . .? Do you not know . . .? Do you not know that the unrighteous will not inherit the kingdom of God? . . . that your body is a temple of the Holy Spirit within you?' (1 Cor. 6). He reproved them for not living up in practice to what they already knew. They had received his instructions as true in their minds; God had spoken to them. It was precisely because they knew these truths that Paul expected them to live accordingly.

We cannot evade this fact : God does not bypass the minds He has given us. Mere hearing will not further our Christian growth. If the Word of God is not constantly informing and shaping our thinking, we cannot expect to advance as Christians.

CONVICTIONS

This is because what we genuinely think and believe governs what we do and become. Mere information will not change us; convictions will. Many people knew that there were millions in China who had never heard of Christi-

[2] *Letters of John Newton*, p. 150.

anity, but they did not go to China to preach Christ. It was Hudson Taylor, with his God-given convictions about the eternal destiny of men without Christ, who went. This is why the Bible warns, 'keep your heart with all vigilance'. The heart there means our whole inner life, including chiefly our thinking. 'Keep your heart with all vigilance; for from it flow the springs of life (Pr. 4 :23). Not manners, but *mind* maketh man.

This is patent in many spheres. Millions followed Chairman Mao because his *Thoughts* gripped their minds and fired their imagination. The story of how Kruschev became a disciple of a different Communism illustrates the same point. Describing his first real introduction to Marxism at the age of 28, he said : 'When I listened to lectures on political economy and the lecturer spoke about the wage system under capitalism, about the exploitation of the workers, it seemed to me that Karl Marx had been at the mine where my father and I worked.' His biographer comments : 'The ideas of Marxism excited Kruschev because they seemed to have been proved true by his own experience.'[3] It was the *ideas* that captured him and gave impetus to his subsequent career and rise to power.

Equally significant are the many today who have no firm beliefs and hold to no absolutes. The result? For them nothing is worthwhile, nothing has lasting worth. On that basis, it is no wonder that little is attempted, little gained.

This same principle of the mind affecting the man is discernible in Paul. It explains why he gave his life to proclaiming Christ. 'We *believe*, and so we speak, *knowing* that he who raised the Lord Jesus will raise us also with Jesus ... *Knowing* the fear of the Lord, we persuade men ... The love of Christ controls us, because *we are convinced* that one has died' (2 Cor. 4 :13,14; 5 :11,14).

[3] Mark Frankland, *Kruschev*, p. 32.

All this drives home one point: the utter necessity of a biblical mind, a mind informed and directed by God through His Word.

FOUR MARKS

What then are the marks of the biblical mind? Out of many we suggest that five are basic.

Motive

The Christian desires to bring glory to God, to reflect well on Him in a world that misunderstands and rejects Him. Yet he cannot honour God if he lives according to his own opinions and values. For this reason he wants to be renewed in the spirit of his mind, from self-concern to God-concern. This transformation can come, as we have seen, only by the renewal of his mind. So the Christian is firmly resolved to grow in the knowledge and love of God from Scripture. He wants God's truth progressively to capture his mind and so turn his will, conscience, affections, memory – his total self - to the glory of God. He welcomes God's authority over him and desires to submit in everything to His only Master and Lord as He speaks in Scripture. 'Oh, how I love thy law!' (Ps. 119:97).

Orientation

A biblical mind grows increasingly God-centred. The Christian has no interest in merely bookish learning; he wants to know and follow the living God. Hitherto his thinking has been orientated to the purely human, the finite, the natural. His standpoint has been what matters to Number One. He did not know it, but he was trying to make sense of God's world as God's creature — but without God.

Now his mind has another orientation. It allows for God, for the infinite, the supernatural. No longer does it keep God at bay; it banks on the reality of the unseen. It begins with God and thinks outward from Him. It adopts God's perspective.

Scope

From this orientation the Christian's mind discovers in Scripture a unified, God-centred outlook on life – the biblical world view. This is the field of view of the biblical mind; it takes in *life*, it surveys the *world*. This does not mean that every or any Christian has fully-fledged wisdom on every human problem. But just as a climber may take in the full sweep of the surrounding valleys and hills from the top of his peak, so the Christian looks at everything from the vantage point of God's revelation. In practice the Christian may not see everything clearly from this position, but that is because of his faulty perception. It does not alter the fact that he is in the only position from which it is possible to see life whole. Only on the ground of biblical revelation may all areas of human endeavour, knowledge and experience be truly known, both in themselves and in their relation to each other.

This is exclusively true of the biblical outlook. 'This all-embracing biblical perspective, which ascribes all things to the power and wisdom of God, is also the only genuine Christian perspective. It alone provides a full and consistent explanation of all the facts of man and the world. No other explanation is (nor can be) free from incapacitating contradictions.'[4] Every other position has a faulty or partial perspective only. In the first place, every individual discipline is self-evidently partial in its scope. Psychiatry is psychiatry, not anatomy; anatomy is anatomy, not sociology; sociology is not literary criticism;

[4] P. E. Hughes, *Scripture and Myth*, p. 28.

political science is not theology. And so on. Each branch of knowledge has its place; but no single discipline or group of disciplines can produce an over-all view of life. Hence, for example, the futility of trying to construct a total view of man on the basis of certain observed characteristics of a mechanistic nature.

In the second place all non-biblical approaches to life are equally defective. They may have many insights which are correct in themselves, but even these become distorted when seen in the wrong light. Humanism, for example, attempts to raise a comprehensive view of life on the foundation of rejecting the One who alone gives life and fills it with meaning. Communism purports to explain life in terms of economic factors, and in so doing denies or neglects moral and spiritual considerations. Roman Catholicism professes to put forward the true Christian perspective, but does so on the basis of a wrong view of authority. Hence its anomalous mixture of truths and error. The deity of Christ is held, but the sufficiency of His once-for-all work on the cross denied. Access to God is taught, but it is re-routed through the priesthood.

Every outlook on life which rejects the biblical one looks at reality from the wrong angle. In consequence, such truths as it may perceive are exaggerated or scaled down; those it does not see are neglected or denied. By glorious contrast, the biblical writers and those who humbly receive their teaching are able in principle to comprehend all of reality that may be known by men. They may do so because they work from what God, the great I AM, the great Reality, has said.

Many today reject such dogmatism out of hand. To them it smacks of arrogance, presumption. It seems to claim, 'We have got God taped, We know It all!' To them it is the death knell of thought and study. By contrast such urge a 'humbler' approach. We should recognize that there is much we do not know yet. For this reason we should keep moving onwards towards greater truth. The first view, on this representation, seems narrow, closed, boastful; the other large, open-minded, humble. In fact the positions are exactly the reverse. 'The theology of indefinitely extended progress towards truth is itself presumptuous because it is based on the assumption that men are going to learn more about God in this life than in fact they are capable of learning.' H. Blamires goes on to assert that 'men are not going to know, intellectually, any more about God in this life than has already been revealed to them . . . The *we-shall-know-later-on* theologian presupposes that the human understanding will in time (yes, *in time*) attain more adequate knowledge of God. The dogmatist has no such confidence in man's powers.'[5]

The Lord certainly has more light and truth than we have yet perceived, but it is to break forth from His Word. This is in fact an enormous incentive to study what God *has* disclosed. God's world view does not come automatically or easily to anyone. It requires continuous application and study both of the Bible and of life in the light of the Bible. But God, having given us His Word and Spirit, has lifted us to His vantage point. He has placed us in a position from which we may come to see life as He sees it. The Christian therefore wants increasingly to have God's vision of himself, the world, life. John Wesley said, 'the world is my parish'; the Christian's outlook is equally extensive.

Clarity

The biblical mind is clear on three points :

First, *the distinction between particular truths and errors*. For instance, to take a vital example, the fact that

[5] *A Defence of Dogmatism*, pp. 18, 19.

Christ died for our sins is a truth, the denial of it (or addition to it) an error.

Second, *the antithesis between truth and error*. Scripture makes it unmistakably clear that we live in a universe of antitheses : God and the devil, good and evil, salvation and judgment, truth and falsehood. This does not mean dualism; it does mean that what is not truth is untruth and what is not the biblical gospel is no gospel. The Christian is aware that all error contains a percentage (often very large) of truth; he is therefore concerned not merely for specific truth, but for the wholeness and purity of God's revelation (*cf*. Acts 20:27). He can be no party to a 'synthetic' approach to truth, to agreement by conglomeration, or to doctrinal ambiguity.

Third, *the crucial nature of this antithesis*. If it is the one gospel alone that leads to Christ, all other views lead away. If truth saves, untruth damns. Speaking once in Berlin, Dr F. A. Schaeffer referred to 'this horrible wall'. The guide on a tour of West Berlin had pointed out that 'the wall is there because twenty years ago some of our own men did not understand the enmity of the enemy'. Dr Schaeffer commented : 'Let us never forget that we who stand in the historic stream of Christianity really believe that false doctrine, at those crucial points where false doctrine is heresy, is not a small thing; this is an *enemy*. If we do not make clear by word and practice our position for truth and against false doctrine, we are building a wall between the next generation and the gospel.'[6] The Christian is not at liberty even to ignore truth, let alone deny or distort it. He is not free to marry it with other views. Men's destinies, the health of the church and above all God's glory are attacked wherever Scripture is not held. This is why the biblical mind has to

[6] 'The Practice of Truth', *Theological Students' Fellowship Bulletin* (Autumn 1967), p. 20.

be ready 'to contend for the faith which was once for all delivered to the saints' (Jude 3). Tolerance is neither virtue nor kindness when it embraces more than God's revelation. The biblical mind is clear about this.

Activity

How may we come in practice to such a mind and outlook? Only by actively seeking to absorb all that God has spoken in Scripture. This life is not long enough for us to exhaust the meaning of His Word (for which reason, incidentally, expository preaching will never run out of material). By His Spirit, however, we may appropriate more and more of the riches of this unique book.

If therefore the Bible is to get into us, we must get into the Bible. And we must get into the Bible in order to get out of it all that God has built in. Some foods are advertised as 'body-building' because they give more than temporary sustenance. Similarly our reading of the Bible is to give us mind- and character-building nourishment. We dare not read the Bible merely to acquire a helpful thought or two to see us through the day. This is equivalent to living on snacks; they may stave off feelings of hunger, but you cannot grow on them. We are therefore always to seek the sense which God has written into each passage; only so will His mind be formed in us. We are seeking the mind of Christ, not just random thoughts, however true. 'The word of God is not to be used as a lottery; nor is it designed to instruct us by shreds and scraps . . . detached from their proper places; but it is to furnish us with just principles, right apprehensions . . . (so that they who study the Scriptures) are taught to make a true estimate of everything around them.'[7] To this end we will study individual books of Scripture : their setting, their particular message, their relevance. We will also aim

[7] *Letters of John Newton*, pp. 81, 82.

to comprehend the individual doctrines of Scripture : creation, atonement, regeneration, judgment, *etc*. But more than this, we will actively seek to assimilate the whole pattern of truth which God has unveiled.

Now many Christians display little interest in the Bible's teaching. This is a contradiction of their new nature, but a sad fact nonetheless. Consequently they can give no coherent explanation even of how Christ saves men by His death, let alone of other truths. Not knowing the doctrine of man, they cannot understand themselves or answer humanists. Being ignorant of the Holy Spirit, they cannot live in His power. In their vagueness about Christ and His death, they do not make Him known.

Other Christians know such truths. For them, however, they are so many distinct entities. They are like unstrung pearls; they are pieces of a jigsaw which have never been assembled. They see many pieces, but no complete picture. Each doctrine occupies a separate pigeon-hole in their minds. Each compartment is true in itself, but unrelated to the others. Now we saw earlier that inspiration refers even to the smallest units of meaning – individual words. But it also applies to the whole Bible as one coherent, integrated unit of meaning. And a biblical mind is known by its growing appreciation of the unity of God's truth. This unity is real, not imagined, written into the Bible by God, not forced onto it by men. Some, of course, have attempted to thread God's pearls onto their own string and so make the Bible support their idiosyncracies. They invariably find that their string is too short; they have to discard or distort some of the pearls. By projecting their own ideas onto Scripture, they never discern the single mind of God which is in and behind it.

Let me illustrate. Sometimes when you read an ordinary book you may take in certain points the author makes. When you finish the book, however, you still have not fathomed how his mind works; you have read him, but not been on his wavelength. Now the Christian obviously wants to figure out each specific truth the Bible teaches; but he also wants to have light on the relation of the parts to the whole and in all this to discern and follow the one mind of God.

This concern does not come from idle curiosity; still less from any ambition to foist his views on the Bible. *Logically* it issues from the fact that all revealed truth comes from God. God holds all truths together. The one divine author gives His book its unity, its pattern, its system of truth. Through the fabric of every passage run the continuous threads of God's mind and being and ways. If the Bible had been given to us by men who were independent of God when they wrote, it would not enshrine this pattern of truth. It *is* there directly because 'men moved by the Holy Spirit spoke from God' (2 Pet. 1 :21). The Christian cannot shut his mind to this. *Practically* the Christian's love for God prompts his concern for an integrated grasp of revelation. If boy loves girl he extracts every last ounce of meaning from her letters. If anyone truly loves God, he cannot remain unconcerned about *all* that God has disclosed for our benefit and His glory. Thus the biblical mind is the mark of a person seeking the living God in all His fullness and majesty.

Such study is exhilarating as well as edifying. It is exhilarating because it is the difference between unstrung pearls and a beautiful necklace; between dismembered jigsaw pieces and the full picture; between isolated chords and the full concerto. To begin to see God and something of the majestic sweep of His truth is the highest privilege and delight given to the mind of finite man. 'How precious to me are thy thoughts, O God! How vast is the sum of them!' (Ps. 139 :17). 'Thy words were found, and I ate them, and thy words became to me a joy and the delight of my heart; for I am called by thy name, O Lord, God of hosts' (Je. 15:16). Such delight is calculated to fire our love for God Himself.

This is *edifying* also. 'It is one of the clearest principles of divine revelation, that holiness is the fruit of truth; and it is one of the plainest inferences from that principle, that the exhibition of the truth is the best means of promoting holiness.'[8] To become aware of how all His truths relate together helps us to have a larger vision of God, to have Him more central in our minds. This is crucial when God, as He is conceived by many Christians, is far too small. Scripture gives a framework to our thinking which helps us to approach every problem, moral or intellectual, from God's perspective. This is why the psalmist wrote: 'Through thy precepts I get understanding' (Ps. 119:104).

Through Scripture God's outlook comes across to us, His perspective becomes ours and His mind is formed in us. As this process goes forward, the Holy Spirit does two things. First He brings us in experience increasingly under the authority of Him who speaks in Scripture. He helps us to please Him in all our thinking and speaking and doing. 'I have laid up thy word in my heart, that I might not sin against thee' (Ps. 119:11).

Second, He shows us more of Christ in all the Scriptures. There we behold the glory of our Lord and are being changed into His likeness (2 Cor. 3:18). This is why we can echo the words of the Ecuador martyr, Jim Elliot. He said of his Bible reading: 'None of it gets to be "old stuff", for it is Christ in print, the Living Word.'[9]

[8] C. Hodge, *The Way of Life*, p. v.
[9] Elizabeth Elliot, *The Shadow of the Almighty*, p. 39.